REALLY???

Stories from Yesterday's Headlines

Compilation and Commentary by
Kate R. Gillett

INLAND
EXPRESSIONS

Clinton Township, Michigan

Published by Inland Expressions

Inland Expressions
42211 Garfield Rd. #297
Clinton Township, MI. 48038

www.inlandexpressions.com

First Edition 2014

Copyright @ 2014 by Inland Expressions

ISBN-13 978-1-939150-06-6

Printed in the United States of America.

Design by Inland Expressions

Table of Contents

Introduction

During the research phase of this book's creation, the author observed a striking similarity between many news reports of the past and those of the present. In fact, a large percentage of the stories included in this work could just have easily appeared in a newspaper purchased today. Of course, there are problems in our current world that were unknown to those living during the previous two centuries, but then again, the opposite is also true as our ancestors faced several difficulties which are equally unfamiliar to us.

The avoidance of incorporating any events of historical significance was a primary determining factor in the selection of stories for this book. Furthermore, each account included in this work has been reproduced exactly it originally appeared. As such, only a minimal amount of corrections or errors has been noted.

In the era before radio and television, the newspaper was the public's primary source of information. Because of this, many of the stories dating before the 1930s are significantly more descriptive in nature than has become the norm in the present.

While assembling the articles used in this book, it was interesting to note the spelling changes of relatively common words over the past century and a half. An example of this is the word employee, which was commonly spelled as employe during this timeframe. Likewise, the general usage of some words has also changed during the same period.

It is hoped that the reader will gain a further insight into daily life at the time in which the following narratives where originally published.

Chapter One
Misadventures in Matrimony

With the capacity to bring out both the best and worst in each individual, marriage is the most complex form of relationship in which two people can enter into. As the following newspaper articles will relate, such relationships were no less complex during the late nineteenth and early twentieth century than they are today. Noteworthy in the following accounts is the level of detail in which people's personal lives were described in newspapers of the day.

In the following story, it appears that there was a lack of Christmas cheer in the Condiff household at Herrick, Illinois during the 1903 holiday season.

HERRICK WOMAN USES HER HATCHET

Pana, Ills., Dec. 24-(Special to The Review)-A woman with her hatchet looking for her husband made a sensation last night at Herrick. A plate glass window was smashed out of a saloon and a door was smashed open.

Mrs. Frances Condiff suspected that her husband was gambling in the saloon. She went to the front door of the saloon with hatchet in hand after closing hours, intending to bring out her husband. The door was locked so she knocked out the plate glass window and got in. Not finding her husband she went to the back door and broke it open. She did not succeed in finding her husband.

The Decatur Review, December 23, 1903.
Decatur, Illinois.

In the next article, a man's wife and sister-in-law take it upon themselves to assault him on a country road in Iowa during the summer of 1905.

BEAT UP BY WIFE.

LeMars, Ia., Aug. 31.-Henry Asal, an elderly German who works for John Behlken, in Preston township, was badly pounded up by his wife and her sister, Mrs. Helmuth Schwiesow. Asal and his wife came from Germany about a year ago and Mrs. Asal went to live with her sister and Asal sought work outside.

Mrs. Schwiesow has done her best to keep the two apart. On Sunday Asal met his wife at the country church and she asked him to come and see her that day and talk over a letter she had received from one of their sons in the old country. Asal proceeded to the Schwiesow farm in the afternoon and met Schwiesow and the two women who were driving in the road near the place. According to Asal's story Helmuth Schwiesow held the horses while the women got out of the rig and assaulted him. Mrs. Asal using a billy which was given to her by her sister. Asal is badly used up. He told his story to County Attorney Struble and warrants were issued for the arrest of the parties, who will have a hearing on Wednesday before Justice Alline.

The O'Brien County Bell, August 31, 1905.
Primghar, Iowa.

While much has been made of the dramatic increase in divorce rates over the past forty years, such events have been a component of our society for a very long time. As the following stories illustrate, acts of violence have also been a common characteristic of these emotionally charged events.

GOT REVENGE.
Woman Shoots Man Who Married and Deserted Her.

Janesville, Wis., April 19.-In the presence of the woman who supplanted her, Florence Dugan shot three times and fatally wounded George Schumaker, who she says had married and deserted her.

The shooting occurred in the principal street during the busiest hour of the afternoon. The woman had just left the district attorney's office after swearing out a warrant for Schumaker's arrest. Still laboring under the emotion with which she had told her story, she almost ran into her husband and the other woman.

He tried to brush past her and she drew a revolver from her handbag crying: "We'll settle this now." The first bullet struck the man in the neck and he fell. Stepping across his body the woman fired two more bullets. She was seized as she was about to fire again.

Schumaker is not expected to live till morning. The woman, who was taken to a cell, expressed no regret. She says that after she married Schumaker he treated her cruelly and forced her to support him by working in a local hotel.

Semi Weekly Waterloo Courier, April 23, 1907.
Waterloo, Iowa.

Corset Saved Her Life.

CLINTON, Ill., special: George Caplinger an inmate of the Soldiers' Home at Quincy, attempted to kill his wife by firing two shots at her. The first shot struck her in the shoulder. The second struck a steel in her corset which saved her life. Caplinger then turned the revolver on himself and inflicted what will probably prove a fatal wound. The couple have six children and did not live harmoniously together before he entered the Soldiers' Home. He came here to effect a reconciliation. Failing in this he attempted to kill his wife and himself.

The Gazette, September 13, 1895.
Cedar Falls, Iowa.

Besides the dangers posed by a vengeful spouse, an individual's safety is equally at risk from the actions of an in-law. As described by the following, such hatred can be unleashed by the most innocent of actions.

POLITENESS MEANT DEATH TO A KENTUCKY DOCTOR.

Birmingham, Ala., Dec. 24.-His politeness cost Dr. John Wheeler, a prominent physician of Berry, his life yesterday when he was shot by his father-in-law, Thomas Kimbrell, a wealthy planter for no act but that he bade him the time of day. For over a year the two men had not been on speaking terms, their differences originating in Kimbrell's objections to the marriage of his daughter to Wheeler.

While Wheeler was returning from a visit to a patient he drove past the country store of William Ray. Ray and Kimbrell were standing in the front door of the store, and as Wheeler approached he bowed and said:

"Good morning, gentlemen."

"I thought I ordered you not to speak to me," replied Kimbrell..with an oath.

At the same time he seized a shotgun which lay just inside the store door and fired both barrels at Wheeler as the rode off. One charge took effect in the doctor's head and the other in the back. Death resulted a few minutes later.

Kimbrell then mounted a horse and fled. A posse is pursuing him, and there is talk of lynching.

The Post-Standard, December 25, 1899.
Syracuse, New York.

There are times in which a relationship's troubles begin long before the marriage ceremony. The following excerpt illustrates one young man's fear of being subconsciously coerced into marriage.

HYPNOTIZED YOUTH FEARS WOMAN'S WILES.

St. Louis, Mo., Dec. 24.-Louis Putnam, a musician, 30 years old, called at the marriage license office and requested the clerk in charge not to issue him a license to wed should he ever ask for it.

"No matter how hard I beg or what reward I offer, don't give me the license."

He went on to state that a young woman had him hypnotized and was determined to marry him. He was bound that she should not. He said she would endeavor to lure him out of the city for this purpose and he had taken steps to thwart her plans. He refused to give the name of the woman. Putnam seemed perfectly rational.

The Post-Standard, December 25, 1899.
Syracuse, New York.

On a happier note, the next story tells of an improbable set of circumstances that brought two people together.

The Egg Brought a Husband.

A proposal came to a pretty Maine school teacher in a very novel manner. While at her father's home in Bidney a few years ago she wrote her name and address upon an egg which she had secured in all its warm freshness from the maternal nest. The egg went to market, and the fact that it bore an inscription was forgotten. In the course of weeks a letter came to the schoolma'am, and to her amazement she learned that that particular egg had hatched strange results. The son of a big commission merchant in a Massachusetts city had seen the name and had written to say that "If the young lady was as pretty as her name he would like to form more intimate acquaintances." With the characteristic modesty of the Maine schoolma'am our heroine discouraged the advances of the strangely acquired admirer. However, he was persistent, and came down to Maine. It is to be supposed that he found his ideal, for an engagement and wedding followed in quick succession.

The Galveston Daily News, January 2, 1891.
Galveston, Texas.

Bigamy is defined as the act of marrying one person while still being legally married to another person. Although such acts still

5

occur to this day, this form of crime was a much more common facet of American culture during the not so distant past. As the following account demonstrates, the incidence of bigamy during this period was assisted by a lack of strict marriage controls in certain parts of the country.

CHECK TO BIGAMY IS URGED

New York, Dec. 27.-Asserting that getting a marriage license in New York was easier than buying a theater ticket, two judges in general sessions today came out in favor of a measure which would require publication of the names of persons obtaining licenses and prohibiting the ceremony for a month. This, it was asserted, would check runaways and bigamy.

"All you have to do to get married in New York," said Judge Talley, "is to go to a window in the municipal building and get a license, and then go to another window and get married."

His remarks were made in suspending sentence on a married man who had contracted a bigamous marriage. Judge McIntyre said 28 persons had been convicted of bigamy here in 1921.

The Washington Post, December 28, 1921.
Washington, D. C.

As the following pair of stories relate, it seems that some husbands are more than willing to carry out phony suicide attempts in an effort to scare their wives. In both cases, however, it appears that these misguided endeavors backfired on their perpetrators.

Husband Feigned Suicide too Often

Alleging as grounds for a divorce the number of times her husband frightened her by pretending to commit suicide, Mrs. Lorean Harmon filed suit Tuesday in Cass circuit court. After every quarrel, she declares, he feigned to have taken various poisons and had her run for the doctor. She alleges he purchased a revolver Saturday and pretended to have shot himself. Three of the cartridges, he told her, were for herself and three for him. She says she fled without calling a doctor this time. Mrs. Harmon's former home was in Burlington, but she now lives in Young America.

Carroll County Citizen-Times, June 16, 1906.
Delphi, Indiana.

FEIGNED SUICIDE.

Hornell, May 7.-Shortly after half past 3 o'clock this afternoon, Charles Hill, jr., eight years of age, residing with his parents at No. 20 Canisteo street, rushed into the police station and stated that his papa had just taken poison and was dying. Officers at once hurried to the scene and found Chas. Hill, twenty-nine years of age on the floor in an apparently unconscious condition and detected the unmistakable fumes of carbolic acid. Coroner Wakely who had been notified from the police station appeared at this instant with a stomach pump and started to pump out the stomach of the prostrate man. He had barely commenced operations when the supposedly unconscious man jumped to his feet and stated the he had not drank any of the poison. When questioned about the matter he stated that he had smeared carbolic acid on his teeth and lips and thrown himself on the floor for the purpose of scaring his wife with whom he had some trouble. The police immediately placed him under arrest and took him to the police station where he is confined on the charge of having attempted suicide. He will be given a hearing in the morning.

Allegany County Reporter, May 11, 1909.
Wellsville, New York.

After taking the plunge into marital bliss, it is occasionally discovered that a mistake has been made. In some cases, this realization may take months, years, or even decades, there are, however, examples in which the gestation period of irreconcilable differences is remarkably brief.

WEDDED TWENTY DAYS AND PART

Anna and Therion Hostetter are apparently convinced that there is more pleasure in pursuit than in possession; at least this may properly be concluded to be true as regards the wife, who, after twenty days of married life, has instituted a suit for divorce against her husband. The couple were married at Marshalltown the 16th day of last March and separated on the 5th of the present month. They came here recently from Marshalltown, where the bride, who is the plaintiff, resided for three years.

"Very soon, within a day or two after marriage," declares one paragraph of the bill of complaint, "the defendant, in violation of his marriage vows and without any fault on the part of the plaintiff, became very abusive towards her."

Cruel and inhuman treatment are the main allegations of the petition.

Semi Weekly Waterloo Courier, April 23, 1907.
Waterloo, Iowa.

There are an incalculable number of reasons for a marriage to become troubled. Wisconsin is known as America's dairy land, and it is from that state that our next story originates.

HUSBAND REFUSES TO BATHE SO HE HAS TO SLEEP WITH COWS
[BY ASSOCIATED PRESS]

Manitowoc-August Eller claims that for more than two years he has been obliged to sleep with the cows in the barn or on a kitchen chair, being prohibited by his wife from entering her bed chamber. This story was related in court when his wife, Minnie, applied for a divorce. Mrs. Eller told the court that Eller had not bathed for two years. The husband admitted that he does not bathe during the winter, but maintained during the summer he occasionally washed in a nearby stream. Besides the charges of uncleanliness, Mrs. Eller charges that he put water in the milk which is used in the household and is generally stingy. The principal charge against Eller is infidelity. This is the third attempt of Mrs. Eller for a divorce. The divorce was granted.

Janesville Daily Gazette, March 28, 1921.
Janesville, Wisconsin.

In the next example, we witness that not even those who have devoted themselves to a life of religion are beyond the power of temptation.

ELOPED WITH THE ORGANIST.

BALTIMORE, Nov 16.-The congregation of Calvary Methodist Episcopal church were shocked Wednesday to learn that their popular pastor Mr. C. M. Bragg, had eloped on Monday with Miss Ianthe Phelps, the organist of his church. Mr Bragg is 43 years old and deserts a wife and family of five children. Mrs. Bragg, who is in delicate health, was under the impression that her husband was in the county on church business till she happened to find a note on his study table with these words:

"I am a ruined man. I am going away and will not return. Tell the children I am dead."

The church authorities held a meeting, but arrived at no final decision. Last week both parties were present at a church social. No one had ever observed any intimacy between them. Miss Phelps sent a postal card to her father saying that she had gone with the clergyman.

The Daily Chronicle, November 16, 1893.
Marshall, Michigan.

As the next two articles demonstrate, fortunes can change dramatically for an individual following the breakup of a marriage. In the first case, we gain an insight into the long memory of a jilted husband. In the second tale, a man respects his spouse's privacy, while his disappearance years earlier had led to another man being buried under his name.

LOVE RETURNS AS FORTUNE CHANGES

New York-This is the story of a couple which shall be nameless, because of the prominence the man has attained.

They had been deeply in love when they married. That was ten years ago. Much has happened in ten years, and in their case they had drifted apart. At first there were little scraps, mended by a kiss and a few loving words.

By degrees the rift became larger. She wanted the comfort, if not the luxuries of life, and told him many times of the motor cars and theater boxes she could have if she had married Tom, Dick or Harry instead of him. Once he used to weave stories of a tomorrow, but tomorrow never came, and finally the friction became too much for him.

The Separation and Sacrifice.

"You are never satisfied," he said after one of these quarrels. "You have no belief in me. Perhaps I don't amount to much. We don't get on. You remain here and I'll find a place for myself. I'll let you have enough to keep you going-$25 a week"

She agreed to this joyfully, and in a few days he had removed to a furnished room not many blocks away. Each week she received an envelope with the stipulated amount in it. Otherwise they lived as strangers.

The man had only left himself enough out of his salary to keep himself alive. There was no overplus for amusements, and his chief recreation was reading at the public library.

The Pencil of Destiny.

One evening, having finished his evening paper, he took up a pencil and began to draw on the edge. He had a sense of humor and was making a comic picture of something he had just read. He was fond of drawing and had given much time to it before his marriage.

Then he took a sheet of paper and drew several comic sketches, and they amused him so much that just for fun he sent one to a comic paper. It was accepted and the editor asked for more. He kept on drawing and in three years had attained a reputation under the name of "Scorn."

The Woman's Interest Revives.

Meanwhile his wife lived on in the old house, perfectly contented and only slightly curious when her allowance was gradually increased. When one day the envelope contained $50 she decided to go after him. She called at the place where he had been employed when they parted and asked to see him. The clerk grinned.

"He left over a year ago."

She rushed to the house where he had roomed. "He left over a year ago." She was informed. Still the $50 arrived regularly.

The Town of Tomorrow.

In California lives a thin man who is something of a cynic. His reputation as a comic artist is established and money comes easily to him. Once a pretty woman asked him why he lived alone.

"I have a wife," he told her. "I left her because she didn't believe in me. I am never going to take her back. It hurts a man to be tied to a bundle of pessimism in petticoats."

"And did she love you?" the pretty woman asked.

"I hardly think so."

Once his agents wrote him that she wanted to know where he lived.

"Tell her," he wrote, "that I am in the Town of Tomorrow." And she understood.

Escanaba Morning Press, May 26, 1915.
Escanaba, Michigan.

HE REVEALED HIS IDENTITY.

Twenty-six years ago George Forbes, then 25 years old, and holding a clerical position in New York, was married at Honeybrook, Lancaster county, to Miss Annie, the 22-year-old daughter of William Bewley. They failed to agree and separated after 18 months, the young wife returning to her father's home with her five-month-old daughter. A few years later, the body of a man, supposed to be that of George Forbes, was buried at Contesville. Mrs. Forbes looked upon herself as a widow. Some years later she married a farmer, and now resides near Berwyn, the mother of two children by her second husband.

STRANGE STORY.

After the separation, Forbes went to Florida and then to San Jose, Cal., where he is now a prosperous fruit grower. He believed all along that his wife had no wish to see him, but at last he could not control his longing to hear what had become of her and his child, and last week he came East. On Saturday, in Honeybrook, he learned that his wife had married again, and he forthwith determined never to disturb her. But when he learned that his daughter was alive, married and living in Honeybrook, he called upon her and revealed his identity, producing the proof necessary to convince her that he was indeed her missing father.

Who the man was who was buried many years ago at Coalesville under the name of George Forbes, will probably never be known.

Lebanon Semi-Weekly News, March 17, 1904.
Lebanon, Pennsylvania.

As related in the following excerpt, not all of the news from the marriage front is necessarily bad.

COUNTY GOES 3 YEARS
WITHOUT DIVORCE SUIT

HARRISBURG, NEB., May 8.-Persistant appeals on the part of Miss May Hyland, chief of the state bureau of vital statistics, for a report on divorces in Banner County for the year 1921, finally elicited the following short and laconic reply from E. D. Wilson, county clerk:

"We love our wives out here. There were no divorces in

Banner county in 1921. I have written you this fact several times in answer to your persistent call. We cannot promise as much for the current year, however, we have one, solitary divorce case on the docket."

Statistical records disclose that Banner county did not have a single divorce in 1919 or 1920.

The county is located in the far corner of Western Nebraska, bordering the Colorado line.

Joplin News Herald, May 8, 1922.
Joplin, Missouri.

Many Hollywood celebrities are renowned around the world for their excessive number of marriages. Few, however, can hold a candle to the subject of our next article.

HOLDS DIVORCE RECORD.

Miss Lizzie McCarty, of Marion, Ind., enjoys the distinction of having been married seven times in nine years. The first husband was Jesse Hammer, whom she married when she was 20 years old, and was divorced from him three months later. Two months later she married him again, and in less than four months got a divorce from him. Her third husband, Lemuel Moore, was sent to the Michigan City prison and she obtained a divorce from him. She moved to Tipton and there married Levi Jack, from whom, in less than a year, she got a divorce. The trouble killed this husband, it is said. The she married Eli Coats at Tipton and lived with him two years, when she got a divorce on account of cruel treatment. She went to Marion and married Ed. Hunt, from whom she obtained a divorce after six months. She resumed her maiden name.

Goshen Daily Democrat, May 2, 1904.
Goshen, Indiana.

The animosity generated between ex-spouses requires little explanation. In many cases, a divorce only signifies the beginning of another period of prolonged conflict. Despite the violence related in

13

previous examples, the next story tells us that not all acts of revenge are intended to cause bodily injury. Charivaris are defined as mock serenades usually played as joke to newlyweds.

GIVES TWO CHARIVARIS
TO HIS DIVORCED WIFE

CHICAGO, June 8-The efforts of a man to make life a burden to his divorced wife and her new husband brought him to a cell in the West Chicago Avenue Station last night. The prisoner is Felix Dombrowski of West Division street. He was caught after a week's search

The first offense was two weeks ago, when it is charged that he hired a brass band to serenade the woman and her husband, Alexander Woglantowski, at their home, No. 840 Milwaukee avenue. After the band had played ragtime melodies, funeral marches were rendered and then discord. The band left only when neighbors turned out to mob it.

On another occasion, Dombrowski hired a number of boys, and provided them with tin pails and cans. He ordered them to go into the hall of Mrs. Woglantowski's home to make a noise. The boy did so, but the annoyed woman armed herself with a broom and scattered the boys.

The Post-Standard, June 9, 1902.
Syracuse, New York.

Chapter Two
The Dangers of Explosives and Firearms

In 1867, a Swedish chemist by the name of Alfred Nobel patented an explosive that became known as dynamite. Nobel's formula represented a significant advancement in safety over pure nitroglycerin; the most commonly used high explosive of the day and a substance, which had the dubious reputation of being highly unstable. Despite this, the improper use of dynamite has often led to catastrophic results. As related in the next few stories, it seems that frozen dynamite was a problem commonly confronted by its users during the late nineteenth and early twentieth centuries. It also appears that many of these same individuals had difficulties associating the danger of applying heat to explosives. Of note in the first two stories is the fact that they appeared in the same edition of *The Indiana Democrat*.

House Blown Up.
By the explosion of 30 sticks of dynamite in Washington township, York county, the home of John Gochenour was blown up and its owner seriously injured. The dynamite was to be used in blowing away stumps, and, thinking it was frozen, Gochenour placed it above the kitchen stove. A few minutes later there was a terrific explosion which wrecked the house.

The Indiana Democrat, November 13, 1907.
Indiana, Pennsylvania.

Dried Dynamite on Stove
Frank Matugle was instantly killed and Peter Mattle and Joseph Carbace were probably fatally injured in an explosion at

Payne, 18 miles east of New Castle. The men were drying dynamite upon a stove. Matugle was standing nearest and his head was blown off.

The two others were so mangled that the they will not likely recover. The accident occurred at the home of Carbace, whose wife was slightly hurt. The men were employed in quarries.

The Indiana Democrat, November 13, 1907.

Indiana, Pennsylvania.

Dynamite Blast Kills Five.

London, Ky.-Five men employed by the Louisville & Nashville railroad, one mile north of Hazelpatch, this county, were killed Monday by the explosion of one hundred sticks of dynamite, which they were thawing.

Grand Rapids Tribune, February 27, 1907

Grand Rapids, Wisconsin.

As the following two articles obtained from the pages of London newspapers will attest, there is ample evidence to suggest that ignorance towards the dangerous combination of heat and dynamite was in no way a phenomenon unique to North America.

EXPLOSION OF CARTRIDGES.

A serious explosion occurred near St. Austell, Cornwall, on December 10, through the recklessness of a foreman of railway works, named Webb. It appears he placed some cartridges of dynamite on the hot plate of the cooking apparatus in his house, and the result was, as might have been expected, that the cartridges soon exploded with terrific force. The house was almost completely levelled with the ground, and, of the four or five persons in the building at the time, one was killed instantaneously and all the others were seriously injured.

The Week's News, December 14, 1872.

London, England.

FATAL EXPLOSION OF DYNAMITE.

A shocking accident occurred at noon on Wednesday, in a small quarry called Chwarel Fawr, on the side of Cefndu Mountain, near Waenfaur, a place distant about six miles from Carnarvon. Mr. Richard Eamesth Eames, the agent and manager, and Richard Hughes, Hendywaenfawr, were in the machine room, engaged in preparing and tempering dynamite. It is supposed that they placed the composition on the stove. By some means it exploded, and although there were but two pounds of it, so great was the force of the explosion that the roof of the place was thrown off and blown to a great height, and everything in the place was shattered to atoms. Richard Hughes received such serious injuries that he died within a few minutes. Mr. Eames was dreadfully injured, and he expired on Thursday, after suffering intense agonies. The explosion caused great alarm among the workmen.

The Sun & Central Press, October 12, 1872.
London, England.

Besides accidents caused by carelessness, dynamite has, on occasion, been put to use for more nefarious purposes. In the following article, a man in the Oklahoma Territory, distraught over the loss of his job, utilizes a stick of the explosive to remove himself from this world.

BLOWS HIS HEAD OFF

Perry, O. T,, March 11.-Knight W. Joles, formerly of Wichita, who was arrested in this city last week for burning United States mails, committed suicide at this place yesterday morning by blowing the upper part of his head off with dynamite. The tragedy occurred on the banks of Cow creek in the northeastern part of the town. Thither the young man had gone at ten o'clock in the morning, and holding the stick of dynamite against his head caused it to explode. The upper half of his head was torn off by the force of the explosion and his hands were badly mutilated.

It its thought that the suicide of Knight Joles was the result of despondency over his arrest and the loss of his federal position. The night before his death, however, his friends were unable to detect anything unusual in his conduct. He appeared to be in good spirits and spent the evening with a young lady.

The Hutchinson News, March 11, 1902.

Hutchinson, Kansas.

As related in the following account, some reports involving Alfred Nobel's most enduring creation have a happy conclusion, despite the potential risk of great harm.

Threw Dynamite On Fire.

Shelbyville, Ind., Aug. 12.-Mrs. William Higgins was engaged in burning trash in her yard. She burned boxes, papers, and then picked up a small wooden box filled with sawdust and threw it upon the fire. A terrific explosion occurred, knocking her down and tearing her clothing to shreds. With the exception of bruises she was unhurt. The box contained several dynamite caps and a quantity of dynamite.

The Odon Journal, August 19, 1904.

Odon, Indiana.

Common sense tells us that experimental work with explosive materials should only be conducted under controlled conditions and within specific safety guidelines. It appears in the following instance, however, that an Italian military officer chose to ignore such a protocol and proceeded with his research in a lodging house.

DESTROYED TEN LIVES
Terrible Explosion of Nitro-Glycerine at Susa, Italy.

TURIN, March 21.-An explosion Friday of nitro-glycerine at Susa, about 37 miles west of this city, destroyed ten lives. The exact cause of the explosion is not known. It is thought, however, that a lieutenant of the Italian army, who lodged in the house where the calamity occurred, was making some experiments with nitro-glycerine and that the explosion resulted. The house was blown to pieces and ten of the inmates lost their lives. Several of the bodies have been recovered.

Oak Park Vindicator, March 25, 1892.
Oak Park, Illinois.

With its potential to be used for both good and evil purposes, the gun represent's not only one of humanity's most important tools, but also one of its most deadly creations. While the users of such weapons should be fully acquainted with its dangerous attributes before handling them, accidents still occur on a regular basis. The next pair of stories relate the details of accidents that should never have happened but reinforce the idea that nothing is ever certain when human beings and firearms are involved.

SERIOUS ACCIDENT WITH FIRE-ARMS.

A sad incident befel Mr. Wood, gunmaker, of Waterloo Road, on December 9. A customer sent a revolver to be cleaned, at the same time cautioning the person by whom he sent it that one of its chambers was loaded. Mr. Wood at once placed the revolver where he thought it safe from all meddlers; but, unfortunately, one of his men seeing it took it in hand to examine it, and, while the muzzle was pointing at Mr. Wood, inadvertently pulled the trigger, thereby discharging the weapon, and lodging the contents-a large-sized bullet-in his master's right groin. In the course of the day the bullet was extracted. Mr. Wood is progressing favourably.

The Week's News, December 14, 1872.
London, England.

Killed Himself While Duck Hunting.

QUINCY, Ill., Nov. 17.-Frank Peters, while duck shooting, accidently shot himself through the heart as he was crawling through a hedge fence. He held the gun by the muzzle and drew it through the fence after him. Deceased was 19 years old.

The Evening Herald, November 18, 1893.
Oskaloosa, Iowa.

Chapter Three
Animal Antics

The misadventures of animals, both domesticated and wild, garner much attention in the newspaper world. This is as true today as it was back during the late nineteenth and early twentieth centuries.

Our first tale relates an event that took place following a judge's acceptance of a monkey in lieu of cash as payment for a legal fine.

"FEE" IS NEARLY FATAL TO JUDGE

LAWRENCEBURG, Ind., Oct. 7.-"A fee" presented in police court nearly proved fatal to Magistrate John W. Probst, 78. James W. Flinn, a traveling horse trader, traded an old horse for a large Rhesus monkey and a galon [*sic*] of whiskey. With a tribe of wanderers Flinn tried to consume the liquor, then wanted to "clean up" on everybody he met. Flinn was arrested and pleaded guilty before Magistrate Probst. He was fined $25 and costs but being without money offered the monkey and buggy as payment for the fine.

The magistrate placed the monkey in a cage and while feeding it it [*sic*] attacked him. He was badly bitten, but managed to kill the animal with a heavy stick.

The La Crosse Tribune, October 7, 1912.
La Crosse, Wisconsin.

The next story relates the mischief created by a pet monkey in New York City following its escape from its owner's automobile.

CHASE FOR RUNAWAY MONKEY

F. Goodman, of the automobile firm of Graham & Goodman, at 55 West Ninety-third Street, went driving yesterday with a pet monkey which he had in the auto on a chain. Just as the machine was being taken into the garage the animal broke away and ran west on Ninety-third Street, pursued by employes [sic] from the garage.

The monkey first ran into Lennon's saloon on the corner of Columbus Avenue and Ninety-third Street and created some alarm among the frequenters of the bar. Some of them said that as it wasn't a blue monkey they felt all right. Others were a trifle uneasy.

Alarmed at the stir it had caused, the monkey then started up the stairs leading to the elevated railroad at that point. Meeting a crowd leaving a north-bound train the animal again sought refuge in the saloon. This time some of those in the saloon were really alarmed and professed to see something blue about the animal.

Finally, when the stairway was deserted the monkey scampered up to the platform pursued by the chauffeurs and a growing crowd. Finding itself pressed hard, the monkey climbed a pillar and gained the roof of the station house. Small boys attempted to follow it, and found themselves caught between two fires. The railway employes [sic] protested from below and the monkey protested from above, throwing missiles at his pursuers.

One boy managed to gain the roof, whereat the monkey ran along the gutter, slid down a pillar at the north end and jumped to the tracks. A southbound train nearly struck it, but the monkey dodged in time. The motorman of a northbound train saw the animal and so scared it by blowing his whistle that the monkey ran back to the platform, where it was captured and returned to its owner.

The New York Times, October 11, 1906.
New York City, New York.

By the very nature of their work, many farmers must interact with animals on a daily basis. As the following stories relate, however, not all of these encounters are without incident.

Attacked by Mad Bull.

Cedar Falls, April 19.-(Special)-F. M. Tuttle, a well known farmer living in Mt. Vernon township, narrowly escaped death on Wednesday when attacked by a mad bull. The animal had the famer down. He called for help, but before it arrived he managed to escape, after being severely butted and trampled. The animal, which is three years old, is very vicious.

Semi Weekly Waterloo Courier, April 23, 1907.

Waterloo, Iowa.

COW SWALLOWS WHIP.

A cow belonging to John Ritchey, near Plymouth, choked on an apple. Mr. Ritchey used a buggy whip to push the obstruction down the throat. Not relishing the treatment the bovine bit off the whip and swallowed a large section. The whip is still in the cow's stomach and the animal is doing as well as may be expected. Some joker will doubtless be moved to opine that henceforth the production of this dairy will be whipped cream.

The Logansport Pharos, November 9, 1906.

Logansport, Indiana.

Mice have a long history of being considered a nuisance by the human race. As the next story relates, however, a miner living in New Jersey discovered yet another reason to hate these rodents at the turn of the twentieth century. It is worth noting that the $5,000 nest egg accumulated by this particular individual is equal to approximately $138,000 in today's money.

Mice Eat Miner's Money

Morristown, N. J., Oct. 23-After working industriously for many years Ignatz Bella, a miner in the Hurd iron mine at Port Oram, managed to lay by $5,000. Bella had no faith in savings banks. Placing $2,750 in one package and $2,200 in another he hid them in his shanty. He thought to add to his hidden hoard and took out the packages. To his horror mice had chewed up

23

the bills. He hurried to the First National Bank of Dover, where he was told that bills in the larger package were useless. Part of those in the other package can be redeemed.

The Daily Gazette, October 23, 1900.
Janesville, Wisconsin.

Throughout history, cats have played a ceaseless, if not welcome, role in controlling the population of rats. This is especially true on farms, where the feline remains one of the best methods to control these pests. The next example relates what occurred when a small community in West Virginia forgot about the cat's contribution in controlling rodents.

Town Banished Cats, Now Overrun by Rats

The little town of Sunshine Valley, W. Va., is overrun with rats and mice as the result of having banished its cats. Huge property damage has been done by the invading army of rodents and traps have been used with only moderate success.

There used to be cats in Sunshine Valley, but owners, moved by a simultaneous impulse apparently, disposed of their pets. Then came the pests, with the feline guard gone, and the losses suffered have been alarming. The few cats still left in Sunshine Valley are watched with jealous care and their owners are importuned for loans.

Newport Mercury, July 16, 1921.
Newport, Rhode Island.

Continuing with our narrative concerning the predator/prey relationship between the cat and rat, the next excerpt relates how effective a small group of felines can be in combating rodent infestations.

Thirteen Cats Killed 231 Rats.

Lawrenceburg, Ind., August 26.-Rat-killing day on the premises of Enos Barrett, a retired merchant, was held yesterday. Mr. Barrett had a quantity of corn stored in a warehouse that was a refuge and feeding place for the rats and a few days ago Jay Cook, of North Vernon, shipped a cage of thirteen Angora cats. Mr. Barrett turned the cats loose in the building and began moving the corn. The rats came out thick and fast and at the end of an hour and a half the cats were worn out. They had killed 231 rats by actual count. Several neighbors have applied to Mr. Barrett for the cats and they will be taken throughout the neighborhood to rid it of rats.

The Daily Reflector, August 28, 1913.
Jeffersonville, Indiana.

It appears that government health officials were so concerned about the spread of plague in New Orleans during the summer of 1914, they placed a bounty upon infected rats. As the $5 dollar bounty roughly equates to $115 in today's money, it is a reasonable assumption that officials had no shortage of rats to test for the disease.

$5 BOUNTY OFFERED FOR INFECTED RATS

New Orleans, La., July 11.-"Any persons finding a plague-infected rat will be given a bounty of $5, provided the rat is properly tagged; where caught, if alive, and where found, if dead."

This reward was offered today by Dr. William C. Rucker, assistant surgeon general of the United States public health service, in charge of the rat-destruction campaign to prevent a spread of the bubonic plague in New Orleans. His offer applies to employes [sic] of the health service, as well as the general public.

Of the 2,330 rodents examined, not one has been found to be infected, it was announced.

No new cases of plague were reported today.

The Galveston Daily News, July 12, 1914.
Galveston, Texas.

25

As described by the following article, there were other pests upon the prairie besides rats and mice.

Bring in Your Gophers.

The last legislature passed a law providing a bounty of 10 cents a head for gophers. The fact is not generally known, for if it were the county auditor's counter would be packed high with gopher scalps. One of the most abundant products of the Iowa prairies is the gopher which can best be harvested by the farmers' boys in the gladsome springtime. In some counties several hundred dollars has been paid for gopher bounty alone, and it is expected that the Black Hawk county boys will get busy just as soon as they know, that the law will liberally compensate them for the destruction of this pest.

Semi Weekly Waterloo Courier, April 23, 1907.
Waterloo, Iowa.

In the next story, we will see how a circus trick involving a horse brought about an unintended, and nearly deadly, result.

LIBELED BY A TALKING HORSE

BERLIN, Germany, March 8.-Butzow, in Mecklenburg, has the distinction of being the first town where an inhabitant has been libeled by a talking horse. Recently a talking horse connected with a traveling circus was instructed by its trainer to select from the audience the woman who was most in love. The intelligent animal sought out an elderly spinster who was present with her fiance, whereas shouts of laughter arose from the audience.

Finally, the fiance, losing his temper, drew a revolver and fired a shot, which he merely intended to frighten the jesters. The bullet struck and slightly wounded a married woman who was some distance off. The victim now claims damages for assault, while the spinster sues the circus proprietor for the insult perpetrated by the talking horse.

The Morning Echo, March 15, 1914.
Bakersfield, California.

Animals have a tendency to get themselves into trouble, often leading to dramatic efforts to rescue them. The next pair of stories relates just such examples.

COW IS RESCUED FROM MINE SHAFT

Austin, Nevada, July 3.-A cow belonging to a local dairyman has been rescued after eighteen days in an abandoned mine-shaft without feed or water. The cow apparently wedged her head into a bucket while at pasture and was thereby blindfolded, which caused her to fall down a thirty-foot incline shaft. After eighteen day's search the beast was found, still alive and still blindfolded. She was taken out and is being nourished back to a normal condition.

The Bismarck Tribune, July 3, 1920.
Bismarck, North Dakota.

100 FARMERS DIG SIX DAYS TO RESCUE DOG

Birmingham, Ala.-One hundred farmers, friends of H. A. Wilson, of this city, laid aside their farm duties six days recently to save the life of one of Wilson's hunting dogs which was caught in a crevasse on the mountain side near Birmingham while chasing a rabbit.

Two friends borrowed Wilson's rabbit hound for a hunt. The dog picked up the trail of a rabbit and the chase led up the mountainside and Br'er Rabbit jumped into the crevasse and disappeared. The dog followed. The hole in the mountain was forty feet deep, which the hound didn't know when it went in. After it had gone two-thirds of the way it found itself wedged in. The impatient hunters whistled in vain. The rabbit rested content a few feet farther on, its exit cut off by the dog. The hunters went back to town and told Wilson.

That night the three came back with shovels and set to work to rescue the dog. An electric flashlight was attached to a long pole and lowered into the hole and the dog's predicament was discovered. Dynamite was resorted to.

Farmers gathered for miles around to assist in the rescue.

27

They labored with picks and shovels and explosives. The third day had brought but little progress and the fourth and fifth days quadrupled the crowd until the scene looked like a railroad camp. Blasts of powder on the sixth day brought the workers with[in] two feet of the imprisoned hound and it was pulled out.

The dog was still alive and feebly wagged its tail to show appreciation. The rabbit had succumbed to hunger.

The workers went back to their tasks and Wilson came back to his business in Birmingham. He says he does not regret the time spent in the rescue work.

The Bedford Daily Democrat, January 16, 1918.
Bedford, Indiana.

During the early 1920s, the patrons of a golf course located in eastern Ontario, Canada may have noticed they were losing a few more of their golf balls than usual. The following story reveals the simple, but humorous, solution to this mystery.

Squirrels Hoarded 91 Golf Balls Lost on an Ontario Course

CARLETON PLACE, Ont, Sept 3-Golf enthusiasts on the local links who had observed that squirrels resident on the course were eyeing them in a peculiar manner, learned the reason today.

Leslie Reynolds announced he had stalked one of the squirrels to a hollow tree and found a cache of 41 golf balls. Search of similar hiding places on the course revealed 50 more lost balls, he said.

Boston Evening Globe, September 3, 1921.
Boston, Massachusetts.

The individual of our next story experienced a memorable event while getting into bed one August evening in 1922. It can be safely assumed that following the night in question, this person never went to bed again without first checking under the covers.

Found Snake In Bed

Chariton, Ia., Aug. 17-To prepare for sleep and find a snake coiled upon his bed was the experience of one of the clerks in the Baker store at Lucas. The serpent, which apparently had a yearning for a more domestic and civilized habitat than its relatives, was sleeping peacefully upon the couch when the man appeared. After a short combat he killed the snake and found it to be of unusual size and of a venomous variety.

Employes [sic] and customers of the store are now wondering where the reptile had been quartering himself during the summer, as the clerk had an apartment over the store.

Adams County Union-Republican, August 23, 1922.

Corning, Iowa.

While intruding upon the wilderness, humans run the risk of encountering aggressive animals. In most cases, individuals caught in such situations will find themselves at a distinct disadvantage. The following tale relates one such example when a person working in the frontier of central Ontario happened to sight a moose. Becoming curious, the writer of this story pressed his luck by following the creature, narrowly escaping serious injury, or death, in the resulting chase.

CHASED BY A MOOSE

A correspondent writing from Mecunoma, Musko[k]a, gives an interesting account of an adventure which he had with a moose, while employed in making a toboggan trail through one of the pine forests in that section of the country. While engaged at work, says the Montreal Witness, he came across a moose yard, and, on looking round, saw one of the "giants of the forest" about fifty yards distant. The story of his encounter is, perhaps, best told in the correspondent's own words:

"After a moment," he writes, "the moose turned and walked behind a hill, which, though not high, was steep. I ran to the top with all speed, hoping to get a view of the lordly creature

29

as he made his way through the bush. I could not see him at first, but, on looking down the steep incline, there he was, not ten yards away. He turned to make off, but, striking his rib against the projecting limb of a small hemlock, he was thrown down and round the tree, and as he rose he faced me.

"It was now my turn to run, for the moose charged at me with crested mane, expressing his rage by a fierce bellow, in turning I stumbled, the ground being very uneven, and his feet nearly came down on me as I dodged among some trees. I tried to strike with my hatchet, the only weapon I had, but did not succeed in injuring my pursuer. With some difficulty I at last got out into the deep snow, where my snowshoes were of more use to me. The moose still pursued me, roaring at intervals, and one who has not heard a moose roar can form but little idea of the terrible bellowing noise. After several attempts to strike me with his front feet he balked and stood about twenty yards away, pawing and roaring. I eagerly seized this opportunity to climb a tree and soon after the animal turned and made off. Of all my adventures in the bush the one I have just related came the nearest to being my death."

Logansport Journal, September 24, 1895.
Logansport, Indiana.

As the man in our next story discovered, angry moose are not the only dangers facing those who ventured into the wilderness during the 1890s.

Chased by Five Cougars.

C. E. Hooper, who has just returned from Tillamook, says that May 5, while carrying supplies into the mountains south of Tillamook, William Ryan was chased by five cougars and forced to take refuge in an old cabin. The cougars stayed all night, making desperate efforts to get at him. In the morning a man with a gun arrived at the cabin and drove the brutes away, killing one, which was a monster, measuring eleven feet eleven inches from tip to tip. Mr. Hooper say that the only mails they have had at Tillamook for the past six months have been packed over the mountains on snowshoes or carried in by sailing vessels.

West Bend Journal, May 29, 1890.
West Bend, Iowa.

Besides their use in controlling rodent populations on land, cats were regularly taken aboard ships to perform similar duties on the high seas. If the following story is factual, the unfortunate demise of one such feline solved a mystery that plagued a sailing vessel after some rats were apparently exposed to a substance that caused them to appear as ghostly orbs.

SUICIDE OF A CAT LAYS BRIG'S GHOST

New York, July 11.-The strange tale of the suicide at sea of the ship's cat, and of how her death solved a mystery which had puzzled the officers for more than four years, was related yesterday when the Maria Lorenzo, a Uruguayan brig, arrived in port from Bahia Blanca with a cargo of bones.

Benito Torres, mate of the Maria Lorenzo, whose veracity is unquestioned, particularly because of his huge size, is authority of the yarn. According to Torres, the narrative has its beginning in the South Indian Ocean, when the brig was in the copra trade.

The Maria Lorenzo was drifting dejectedly in a night of inky blackness when suddenly a number of bright phosphorescent lights appeared on the deck. They came apparently out of space and scampered in jig-jag fashion within a few feet of two Lascars at the wheel, who tumbled precipitately down the hatchway. For the remainder of the voyage the Lascars refused to work on the deck at night. The strange lights were seen on several occasions after that.

On reaching Colombo the entire crew deserted. So difficult was it after that to ship a crew that the skipper often was compelled to clear short-handed.

Before leaving Babia Blanca on the recent voyage a big cat

31

was shipped as mascot. She was recommended for her ability to kill rats, but on the first night out she climbed into the rigging and stayed there. On the following day the crew fed her some rum. When darkness fell she was as drunk as any sailor. The will-o'-the-wisps had no terror for her and she careened about the deck trying to catch them.

The officer on watch was suddenly brought to life by a loud screech. All the ghostly lights, except one, disappeared. There was a swish as the cat leaped for the railing and a loud splash as she struck the water, a suicide. On the deck was a wriggling mass of phosphorescent light.

"Somebody went up and touch it with his toe, and what do you think it was?" said Torres. "It was a rat-a phosphorescent rat."

The Galveston Daily News, July 12, 1914.
Galveston, Texas.

The next account describes the bedlam caused by a cat that found itself homeless after the establishment at which it resided was closed down. Apparently, the resulting turmoil caused by this feline was ample enough to warrant a nearly 1,000-word write up in a San Antonio newspaper.

ALL HOUSTON AROUSED OVER ANTICS OF A CAT

Houston, Tex., Jan. 26.-A cat has served to disturb the equanimity of Houston for the last week. It has caused the fire department to make three runs, has been the subject of repeated investigations and complaint on part of the Humane society, has aroused President W. W. Dexter of the Texas Humane society to a special line of investigation, has caused the filing of complaints with the police, the subject of discussion by the Houston commission and a good deal of cursing by private citizens

That one cat could be the cause of so much annoyance, and bring about such activity on the part of the city government, was not before realized. This one is a "Tom" or was at last accounts, but it may be dead by this time. It was the mascot of the Standard theater, corner Milam and Prairie streets, a vaudeville and dance hall, which under the orders of police was closed two weeks ago.

For the last several years the cat was an inmate of the theater and was pampered and petted and knew never a care. It is said to have contracted an appetite for beer that entirely displaced its former liking for mice.

The trouble with the cat came at the time of the closing of the theater. It had enjoyed its daily portion of the beverage and attending the excitement of the closing of the house it managed to get through an attic hole of the third story on to the roof. How this was done is something of a mystery to the public, and also, seemingly, to the cat for it has not been able to get down again.

It was missed for a week before the real stress of anxiety began. Then the cat began yowling [sic] and such cries had never been heard on a back fence or a kitchen roof at night. It would approach the eaves of the roof and look down into the street uttering wild yowls. Its cat face was as cadaverous as an animal's face could be. The eyes sunken and green blazes seemed to emanate from them in the moonlight.

Business people in the vicinity were disturbed, their nerves being affected by the continuous cries of the starving animal. There was no way through the building to the roof for human beings nor could a ladder of sufflcleut length be procured by those directly interested in the cat to go to its relief. Complaint was made to the President Dexter of the state Humane society, to the police and finally to the city commission.

The ladder section of the fire department was at length called out. It made a run to the building, hoisted the extension ladder, and two firemen went to the top of the roof. It was there ascertained that the cat had a wide range over which to roam as it could leap on other buildings but apparently from the roofs of none of them could it find a means of getting to the ground.

Efforts were made to catch it, but it was as wild as a jugar [*sic*] in a jungle and could not be approached. The firemen put in a half hour chasing it and it then crawled through a small hole in a cupola like ornament which made all further efforts to get it useless.

Complaints were so many that the following day the hook and ladder brigade was again called out and another effort made to rescue the cat. The result was the same as on the previous day. Yesterday a third attempt was made by the fire department and Fire Chief Tom O'Leary himself was one of the detail that went to the roof. The cat was wilder than ever. Its former fat sides were gaunt and its eyes blazed with demoniac fire, reminding the chief of Poe's black cat story. The effort entirely without satisfactory result.

The cat still remains on the top of the building and there is considerable speculation as to how long it will it keep up its disturbance before succumbing.

Two plans are now under consideration of the city commission, the chief of the fire department, the Houston division of the Human society, the police department and interested citizens. One is a proposition of carrying food to the top of the building each day or so to relieve its distress. This is not sanctioned by Chief O'Leary who argues that the hook and ladder brigade has other duties than the daily running of several blocks and the mounting of a tall building to feed a cat on the roof. The plan is regarded favorable by others, but insomuch as the brunt of the trouble would be on the fire department Chief O'Leary's position will doubtless rule.

The second proposition is to go gunning for the cat, take a well-loaded shotgun to the roof and end its career. This would be adopted but for the popular superstition of ill-luck in the killing of a cat. None of the fire department boys care to do the job and no policeman has yet volunteered for the service.

One authority advances the idea that the kitty will yet live to trouble that portion of the business section for 29 days, as he is sure it can go without food or drink for 45 days, it having already put in sixteen days of fasting. Conclusions will likely be reached with the next few days upon some sure line of procedure, for popular clamor for relief from the nerve-racking disturbance in the vicinity of the building must be appeased.

The San Antonio Sunday Light, January 28, 1906.
San Antonio, Texas.

The preceding story appears to have a happy conclusion, however, as one week later *The San Antonio Sunday Light* reported the arrival of a former theater employee from Dallas whom had learned of the cat's plight. After locating the hole the cat used to reach the top of the building, the former employee enlarged it and placed some food and water on the rooftop. With the opening now clear, it was believed the trapped cat would find its way to safety. The lack of any further reports concerning the stranded animal leads to the assumption that all worked out satisfactorily.

Prior to the widespread use of motorized vehicles, society relied heavily upon work animals. In the next account, we get a brief glimpse into the importance placed upon these creatures by some municipalities.

HORSES TO GET VACATION

Philadelphia, Jan. 16.-A two week's vacation for every one of the 800 horses in the employ of the city police, fire and street departments will be granted next summer. An infirmary for dumb animals has raised $15,000 to meet the cost, and a committee is at work figuring out how the horses can be spared from their work.

The Bedford Daily Mail, January 16, 1913.
Bedford, Indiana.

Believing that the city in which they lived was derogatory for his two burros, this short article phoned into *The Bedford Weekly Mail* describes the decision by an opera house owner to provide his animals with a sabbatical.

Won't Get Lonesome.

Manager Johnson, of the opera house, has shipped his two white burros to Bloomington where they will summer. "Chip" evidently believes the moral atmosphere of wicked Bedford is not fit for donkeys, and that "Klondyke" and "Alaska," his two pets, will be benefitted by a few months in a city of higher education.-Telephone.

The Bedford Weekly Mail, April 14, 1899.

Bedford, Indiana.

Our final installment presents a humorous incident that took place in a small Nebraskan town, and one in which the animals involved can be considered nothing more than victims of circumstance.

He Wanted Oats But He Got Cats

Neligh, Neb., Dec. 29.-The substitution of a lower-case letter "c" for the letter "o" in an advertisement in the Sioux City, Omaha and local newspapers has caused John C. Trothers, a grain merchant here all kinds of trouble.

Trothers, wishing to replenish his supply of oats, concluded to advertise. Writing his advertisement on a typewriter, he manifolded it and sent copies to the newspapers as follows:

"Wanted-Delivered on track at Neligh 10,000 bushels of cats. Will pay highest market price."

Not noticing the error he awaited results, which came sooner than he expected. With a week cats of all kinds and description commenced to arrive consigned to Trothers. Some were sent prepaid and other collect. They came from the east, the west, the north and the south. The agent of the Northwestern road became alarmed. He was being swamped by cats and wired the superintendent for instructions. That official not knowing what else to do wired back:

"Release all cats not accepted."

Still cats continued to arrive, and still Trothers refused to accept the felines, but his troubles did not end there. Boys about town had learned that he was in the market for cats. They commenced to catch the strays and take them to his place of business. Some days last week he refused as many as 500 cats brought in by boys and three and four times as many coming by rail.

It is estimated that fully 5,000 cats have been shipped into Neligh, and the end is not yet. They are becoming a nuisance and the city is about to take action and order a slaughter of the animals.

The Portsmouth Times, December 31, 1910.
Portsmouth, Ohio.

37

Chapter Four
Criminal Mischief

In our modern world, a number of broadcasting mediums developed over the past century have joined the traditional newspaper in delivering our daily news. These newer forms of communication include radio, television, and the internet. Regardless of the communication method, however, criminal activity constitutes a large portion of the stories reported by a news service. Proving as true today as it was a hundred years ago, such stories will most assuredly remain one of the most popular items reported by the media for the foreseeable future.

Today, the World Wide Web is abounding with frauds seeking to separate unsuspecting victims from their financial assets. Such swindles, however, are just the latest incarnation of deceitful practices that have thrived throughout history. While the following examples of fraud took place during the late nineteenth and early twentieth centuries, they are, in many ways, not unlike those still perpetrated on a daily basis throughout the world.

Lightning Rod Swindlers.

A company of lightning rod men "worked" a couple of Germans in Grant Township, near Corwith, one for $185 and the other for $100 in notes. The parties claim the rod men made false statements to them to induce them to allow the work to be done, and then enforced settlement with a revolver. They claim to work for Call Bros. of Sioux City. They immediately set out to get even with them and caught up with them at Corwith, had them arrested, o[n] warrants issued for the gang, four in number, but not the one who did most of the business. The two who were caught returned the $100 note, paid a light penalty and were released. It seems to take a large amount of experience and newspaper admonitions to educate people along this line, and yet not entirely succeed.

The Gazette, September 13, 1895.
Cedar Falls, Iowa.

A Bold Swindler.

Richard C. McCune, of Marshalltown is said to have cheated Mrs. W. T. Smith out of money which she paid him for the carpenter work and material for her new house. McCune had taken the contract and agreed to pay for the material. He collected nearly $500 from Mrs. Smith, which, instead of applying to this purpose, he put in his pocket and has left the city. Mrs. Smith will have to pay this amount over again or lose her house.

The Gazette, September 13, 1895.
Cedar Falls, Iowa.

A THOROUGHBRED SWINDLER.

CHICAGO, May 4.- O. B. Eshlman, who, by personating his uncle, Reuben Eshlman, a well-to-do merchant of Mount Pleasant, Ia., induced the Malone Pants Company, of Malone, N. Y., to send him on credit 300 pairs of fine pants, was arrested here today as a traveling dealer in pants. Eshlman made a brilliant success, disposing of the whole stock through Northern Illinois at fancy prices. With the proceeds he went into wheat at Chicago, but at the wrong time, losing $1,500 in a day. He stole a ride to Council Bluffs, Iowa, and joined the Salvation Army; was made captain within two weeks, then got drunk and was dropped by the army just twenty-four hours before detectives reached the town. At Dubuque he made enough money as a vendor of alleged eyewater and tooth powder to bring him to Chicago. The culprit had employment on a lake steamer and was about to leave port when officers found him. Eshlaman has been out of the penitentiary only since last fall, when he completed a two-year sentence in

Missouri for attempting at St. Joe to indulge without funds his penchant for pantaloons.

The Salt Lake Daily Tribune, May 5, 1889.
Salt Lake City, Utah.

PAINTED SHEEP.

There is on trial before Judge Drummond an action of S. G. Paul, of Kane county, Ill., against Joel Valentine, John Stewart and others, to recover for an alleged breach of warranty on sheep. It would seem, according to the plaintiff's attorney's say so, that Mr. Paul is the owner of a considerable farm in Kane county, is something of a stock raiser, and a prominent man in the county. The defendants sold to him an undivided half of thirty-four sheep and one ram, represented to be the thoroughbreds from Hammond's stock of Vermont. It is claimed that these were ordinary sheep worth from $4 to $6 or $8 each (the ram being worth less than four cents), all of them being doctored in Vermont to represent Spanish breeds, first by the process of stubbing, which means that in the process of shearing wool was left upon the hide to apply on the next crop; and, secondly, by a process of painting with tar and turpentine, to represent the greasy and colored appearance of the original stock.

The Defiance Democrat, February 25, 1871.
Defiance, Ohio.

Released From Jail.

ADRIAN, Nov. 16.-Vanderpool and Latimer, the piano swindlers, who by sharp work got a note from Farmer Sutton of Medina for $480 last Friday, were released from jail Wednesday. They surrendered the note and thereby obtained their victim's promise not to appear against them. They recently got out of a similar racket in Pontiac.

The Daily Chronicle, November 16, 1893.
Marshall, Michigan.

CLAIMED TO BE A NUN.

"Sister Mary Francis," who claimed when arrested on the charge of larceny that she had been a member of the Sisters of Charity for the past 20 years, was arraigned before Judge Duff in the Municipal Court this morning.

The woman was arrested as the result of the notice "that a fraudulent nun had been making collections in the North End." When arrested she have the name of Marguerite Charpentier, and she was charged with larceny of $3.81 from persons unknown. She was represented by counsel, and Paul Spain appeared for the prosecution.

She told the court that she was a member of the third order of St. Francis. Evidence was introduced in the form of a letter by Bishop Northup of South Carolina written 10 years ago in which Mother Charpentier was authorized to collect money for a Franciscan Mission, but that the permission had since been withdrawn and the mission closed.

Judge Deff declined jurisdiction in the case and held the woman for the grand jury in $300, which she furnished.

Among the interested persons in court at the time of the hearing was Rev Fr Bulter, pastor of St. Ann's Church, Somerville, in whose parish the woman lives.

Boston Evening Globe, July 1, 1915.
Boston, Massachusetts.

The next pair of tales demonstrates how smooth talking thieves can gain a victim's confidence by impersonating a person with respectable credentials in order to orchestrate a criminal act.

CLEVERLY DONE

NEW YORK, May 23-John S. Ward, general manager of Ward & Johnson's carriage repository in Newark, is looking for the man who called at his place of business on Saturday, ordered a neat physician's turnout, informed him that he needed medical treatment, and visited his house yesterday to administer such treatment.

Mr. Ward has reported to the Newark police that while the alleged doctor was applying the treatment, which consisted of pasting strips of adhesive plaster on his back in the form of an asterisk, his fingers were busy in removing from the clothing of the patient a diamond shirt stud, a gold watch and chain and $50 in money.

The man for whom the police are asked to hunt calls himself "Dr. Colder."

The Lowell Sun, May 21, 1904.
Lowell, Massachusetts.

BOGUS NOBLEMAN

New York, May 10. Two hundred dollars in good American money was handed out to a bogus nobleman by the clerk of a well-known Fifth avenue hotel. The "nobleman" has not been heard from since, although he left his luggage checks at the hotel and had made inquiries concerning a suite of rooms. But after receiving the money in exchange for a 1,000-franc note he evidently changed his mind.

Arriving at the hotel the man gave the name Count Hatzfield and said he was a friend of Count Mansfield, who is to marry Miss Nora Iselin, daughter of C. Oliver Iselin, today. This statement gave him the desired entree and his note was readily cashed. Later examination showed it to be a forgery.

Allegany County Reporter, May 11, 1909.
Wellsville, New York.

During the latter part of the nineteenth century, the purchase of life insurance became popular in the United States. Many of those purchasing such policies had little knowledge on the workings of insurance. From the following account, it appears that certain questionable elements of society wasted little time in cashing in on this excellent opportunity.

WILD CAT INSURANCE

SEDALIA, MO., April 17.-C. P. Ellerbe, of St. Louis, attorney of the State Insurance Department, is about to begin proceedings against the Southwestern Mutual Benefit Association, of Sedalia, for attempting to carry on the life insurance business in violation of the State laws. This company was organized in January, and almost immediately fell under the condemnation of the Insurance Department. Superintendent Williams says: "It is, in plain English, a life insurance company without capital, and has no authority to do business in Missouri. Its own leaflet condemns it. It puts total extreme cost of membership at $280, and yet at the end of ten years for $280 paid, they promise to give you $1,000. The experience of centuries proves this to be impossible. No lapses can fill this gap. The whole history of the [sic] life insurance in this country and Europe proves the fallacy of such a promise."

No action will be taken against any bonafide benevolent or charitable association insuring its members on the mutual plan, as was done some years ago. The Legislature, in 1881, enacted that such associations shall not be subject to the general insurance laws of the state. Under the enact the Masons, Odd Fellows, Legion of Honor, and other societies having insurance as an incidental feature, are exempted from the conditions placed upon companies organized to carry on business of life insurance, pure and simple.

The Saturday Herald, April 21, 1883.
Decatur, Illinois.

Petty theft represents what is perhaps the most trivial of all criminal endeavors. As the following stories relate, however, even this form of crime can bring out the worst in people.

THEFT AT ITS LOWEST TERMS.

Richard Richardson was last night locked up at station 5 on the charge of having stolen a dipper containing a few pennies, the gift of charitably disposed persons to an aged woman who sat on the curbstone at the corner of Washington and Lenox streets in the almost zero weather, and ground out questionable harmonies from a weatherworn organette.

She was muffled up in an old tattered shawl, and the gaping seams in her shoes showed the absence of proper foot covering. Many people passed her by during the evening, and those who designed to look upon her with charitable commiseration and dr[o]p a penny for charity's sake in her little half pint tin dipper were few. From lines in her careworn and poverty pinched face one could see that the poor old woman had once seen better days.

She was bitter cold and was often compelled to stop and leave a tune unfinished to warm her hands beneath her scant wrappings. Tears stole down her withered cheek as with her trembling hand she urged an apology for the miseriere [sic] from the organette, and she had just bowed a "thank you, madam," to a richly-attired woman who had tarried long enough to drop a bright new nickel done among the black pennies in her dipper, and was about brushing the tears away f[r]om her face, when, it is alleged, Richardson sneaked along and stooping as if to contribute to the old lady's mite snatched the dipper and fled. He had not gone far, however, when the officer overtook him and he was left in a station 5 cell to medi[t]ate over his career from the time when his mother had, probably, stroked his head lovingly, down to the present.

The Boston Sunday Globe, November 6, 1887.

Boston, Massachusetts.

ALLEGED CHURCH THIEF HELD
IN CHARLES-ST JAIL

Harry A. Dale, who is listed as a church thief and poor box robber in the Bureau of Criminal Investigation, was arrested just before 1 o'clock yesterday morning in the North End by policemen Lett and Lydon. He is known in Providence and Hartford as well as in Boston. He appeared before Judge Burke in the Municipal Court yesterday and was committed to

Charles-st Jail in default of $3000 bail.
The Boston Daily Globe, April 27, 1918.
Boston Massachusetts.

While the perpetrator of the next crime managed to conduct his deed without causing any physical harm to the occupants of the house broken into, the resultant suffering was no less cruel.

MEANEST MAN STEALS STOVE

Canton.-This is the story of the man who deserves the blue ribbon among "the meanest men."

Harry Johnson, 317 George street, reported to the police that while he was at work some one entered his house and stole his stove while the thermometer was registering about zero.

"Br-r-r," said Johnson, with a shiver over the telephone, by way of greeting when he called police headquarters. "S-s-s-s-s some one has stolen my stove."

The police hastened to get a detailed description of the missing stove with its Bertillon measurements, and then dispatched a sleuth to trail the stolen heater and put it back on the job of warming the Johnston's home.

Aside from learning that the fire had first been removed from the stove before the theft, police were unable to obtain any clues.
Atlantic News-Telegraph, January 30, 1912.
Atlantic, Iowa.

The circus in meant to bring enjoyment to the all those who attend, and is therefore billed as entertainment for the entire family. As such, performers of these shows commonly maintain an appearance of cheerfulness as they conduct their acts. From the following account, however, we gain an insight into why one circus performer had little to smile about one summer morning in 1905.

45

DIAMOND IS STOLEN AT CIRCUS

While Frank L. Weaver, one of the circus performers, was absent from the dressing tent for a short while this morning, a sneak thief entered the tent and made off with a diamond ring, valued at $900 and a diamond and opal ring valued at $25.

At the time Mr. Weaver was looking over his wardrobe and had removed his vest, to which was attached his watch chain and on which were the two rings. He was called out of the tent for a short while and during his absence the rings were taken.

The corps of detectives who are with the show, as well as the local police, are working on the case.

The Standard, August 4, 1905.
Ogden, Utah.

As with the preceding example, the next narrative also describes the robbery of a clown. In this case, however, the method used was significantly more violent.

CLOWN ASSAULTED.
Found in a Dying Condition Outside His Dressing Tent.

CINCINNATI, Sept. 27.—Fred Lamont, a well known circus clown travelling with Robinson's show, is lying at the point of death at Terrace park, near this city, from injuries received at the hands of a robber. When it was time for him to appear at the exhibition given Tuesday night at Winchester, Ind., he was missing. A search discovered him lying outside his dressing tent with his skull crushed and his money belt missing.

The Fort Wayne News, September 28, 1894.
Fort Wayne, Indiana.

While the previous pair of examples told tales of clowns being the victims of crimes, the following relates how another of these performers thought he could get out of supporting his child by working for a traveling circus. Although proving successful for more than a year, the scheme finally unraveled during a parade announcing the festival's arrival in town.

CLOWN ARRESTED
Wife Had Not Seen Him For More Than a Year.

Elmer Bohm, one of the clowns with Ringling Brothers circus, was arrested Tuesday morning by Constable Charles Krabill on a charge of non-support, after his sister-in-law had recognized him in the parade. Bohm arranged to pay $2 a week toward the support of his minor child.

Mrs. Bohm, who is employed in this city, had not heard from her husband since a year ago last February. When the parade came up Main [S]treet her sister recognized one of the buglers as Bohm. She at once reported her discovery to her sister, who had the husband arrested. Bohm was easily recognized at the show ground as he has one stiff leg. He is the clown who wore a [M]other [H]ubbard gown.

The Mansfield News, June 30, 1915.
Mansfield, Ohio

The next account describes the violence of a mob directed at the workers and patrons of a street carnival in Cleveland, Ohio during the spring of 1916.

STREET CARNIVAL IS ATTACKED BY A CLEVELAND MOB

Cleveland, April 29.—Twenty men were injured late last night in a riot which occurred when a mob of men and boys attacked a street carnival show at St. Clair avenue and East 53rd street, and wrecked it. Two policemen on duty fought the mob without effect until the arrival of reinforcements when the assailants were dispersed after many had been severely clubbed.

Performers and men, women and children among the spectators at the carnival were attacked by the mob, the leaders

47

of which are being hunted by the police.

The cause of the riot is unknown to police.

The Newark Advocate, April 29, 1916.

Newark, Ohio.

Thievery knows no bounds, but the goods stolen in the next article must certainly rank as one of the most unusual to appear in the pages of a newspaper.

'SWEET TOOTH' THIEF AT WORK HEREABOUT

Of all the thieves who ever made a practice of living off the labors of others there is a brand of thief in Connersville, or the city's vicinity that stands alone in his profession. He is a thief who fears not the sting. He is a thief who has a "sweet tooth." As reports indicate the thief went into the orchard at the George Ostheimer farm and carried away live, buzzing bees. Some of the bees were killed outright, how none knows. 180 pounds of honey were taken and the swarm of valuable bees were about destroyed. John G. Krasser, former councilman and a man who devotes much of his time to bee culture, has advised the thief and any other who might contemplate stealing honey from hives, that the swarm at the Ostheimer farm now has just enough honey to provide food for winter. Other swarms in other places are similarly situated.

Mr. Krasser asks the thief to be humane, not to take the last bite of honey from the bee's mouth. In concluding an announcement Mr. Krasser said: "Mr. Thief, please let the bees have the honey that is now left them if you, or your family, want any honey next year. Don't slaughter the goose that provided the golden egg."

Connersville New-Examiner, October 10, 1921.

Connersville, Indiana.

The motives for the criminal acts described in the next two accounts are uncertain, but both instances involve highly unusual circumstances.

GOLDEN LOCKS SHORN.

Mason City, Ia., Aug. 29.-A daring act was committed at the Nels Jensen home in Grant township, in which little Ruby Yokom, the 13-year-old daughter of Mr. and Mrs. Smith Yokom, a neighbor, who was spending the night at the Jensen farm, was deprived of her fine golden head of hair. About midnight some one entered the bed room of the little sleeper, by prying off the screen and reaching her bed supposed to have chloroformed her, then proceeded to use the shears or a knife, the latter more likely from the nature of the work. For some reason the marauders became alarmed and retreated, as the hair was left on her pillow. The family were not aware of what had occurred till next morning. Ruby presented a sorrowful appearance. Her eyes were swollen and heavy and she suffered a severe headache and besides her glory of hair was gone. A small contusion over her eye leads some to believe she might have been stunned by a blow although she has no knowledge of anything. An examination by a physician followed who gave it as his opinion that chloroform was used, although she might have been struck. No clue to the perpetrators of the act is obtainable.

The O'Brien County Bell, August 31, 1905.

Primghar, Iowa.

GIRL'S HAIR CUT OFF; STORY PUZZLES POLICE

MARION, Ind., Dec. 31.-The police are puzzled regarding the story told them by Miss Ethel Stackhouse, 15 years old, who is a visitor at the home of Mrs. L. G. Graves on the West side. She declares that while she was alone in the house last night a man entered, seized her and with a knife cut off a braid of her hair. When other members of the family returned home the police were called. An investigation disclosed that outside the fact that the girl's hair had been cut there was no evidence of a struggle, and nothing in the house had been disturbed. Miss Stackhouse was badly excited and the police have been unable to obtain a connected story from her as to the man's appearance or how he entered and left the house.

The Indianapolis Sunday Star, January 1, 1922.
Indianapolis, Indiana.

As technology has advanced throughout history, so has the sophistication of criminal activity. Proving to be no exception, the arrival of the automobile sparked the new crime of auto theft, which has grown to the point that a vehicle is stolen every 30 seconds in the United States. The following stories relate a pair of early vehicle thefts that had interesting conclusions.

ALLEGED THIEF CAPTURED
Farmers Riddle Auto With Shot Until Man Quits Chase

Harrisburg-Edwin B. Howell, late of New York, is in jail here charged with stealing an automobile at Gettysburg and glad to be safe and secure within four stone walls.

Howell ran out of funds in Gettysburg on his way to Baltimore. Eugene Snyder of Two Taverns, visiting in Gettysburg, saw the stranger drive away in his car and telephoned to farmer friends along the road.

When Howell found his way barred by farmers at Two Taverns, he tried to run through them and they riddled the car with buckshot. Then they pursued him in other cars, blazing away as often as they got close enough. Eventually Howell's nerves gave way and he ran into a cornfield where the farmers rounded him up and brought him here to jail.

Indiana Weekly Messenger, November 10, 1921.
Indiana, Pennsylvania.

MYSTERIOUS THIEF RETURNS CAR STOLEN
FROM ALGONIAN

Guy Smith's car was taken from his home Saturday night at 11 o'clock, but was returned next morning at 4 o'clock. Who took the car is not known. The sheriff was called, after the car was missed, and telephone calls were sent to nearby towns in an effort to catch the thief. Mr. Smith was in bed at the time, with neuritis. The fellow who used the car did such a slick job of returning it that he was not discovered.

Kossuth County Advance, April 20, 1922.
Algona, Iowa.

Prior to the automobile, the horse was the primary mode of transportation in the United States. Therefore, it is not surprising that horse theft was a common occurrence during this era. The extent of this activity was such that some law enforcement agencies commissioned specialized detectives to recover stolen animals.

HORSES ARE STOLEN

Stephen, a son of Henry Stalcup, who resides one mile north of Elnora, attended church Saturday night at Elnora and while worshipping God some one stole Stephen's horse. Upon discovering his loss he borrowed a horse from Thomas Hastings and, accompanied by Dode Adams, went in search of the missing animal.

Upon reaching the Belleview church, in the Marsh, they discovered the stolen horse hitched to a fence. The two young men lay in wait for the man who had taken the animal and when the services were finished a man walked up to the horse and commenced to untie the halter. While thus engaged young Stalcup grabbed him, intending to make him a prisoner and turn him over to the authorities, but the man jerked loose and made his escape in the darkness.

For some time people attending church in Elnora township have been annoyed by persons stealing their horses.

The Bedford Mail, April 14, 1899.
Bedford, Indiana.

STOLEN HORSE FOUND BY
HORSETHIEF DETECTIVE

John Miller, head of the Cass County Horsethief Detective association today notified the police he had picked up a stray horse which he found wandering near his brother's farm about six miles south of the city.

Logansport Pharos-Reporter, November 12, 1913.
Logansport, Indiana.

Due to their gruesome nature, it is understandable that murders would be among the most commonly reported crimes in the media. The following examples prove that murder was no less violent in the past than it is today.

Working Girls Charged with Murder.

ANNISTON, May 13-In a general row among the female employes [*sic*] in a cotton factory here, a young woman named Rosie Brown was jumped upon and kicked so badly that she died a few hours later. Ten of the girls have been arrested on warrants charging them with murder.

Logansport Daily Reporter, May 13, 1892.
Logansport, Indiana.

SULLIVAN, Ind., special: James Ward murdered his father-in -law, Aaron Hunter, and brother-in-law, John Hunter, cutting off the heads, kicking them around like a football. Ward was pursued and just as he was about to be captured took his own life.

The Gazette, September 13, 1895.
Cedar Falls, Iowa.

HUNT WOMAN TO CLEAR MYSTERY

New York, December 30-Detectives working on New York's latest trunk mystery, today began hunting for a woman who is believed can reveal both the identity of the murdered man and the murderers. To this woman, the police think, belonged the skirt and shirtwaist which were found under the body of the victim in the trunk when it was opened in front of 47 Pitt street, in the heart of the Ghetto, yesterday.

Friends of John Kremenz, a souse wrecker, employed by J. F. Donovan, a contractor, visited the morgue and told the officials there that the dead man resembled Kremenz, who has been missing for several days.

By noon the police were virtually certain that the dead man was Kremenz or Kremen, as he was also known. Michael Molley, a teamster, and former roommate of Kremen, identified the body by a scar on the shoulder.

Logansport Pharos-Reporter, December 30, 1913.
Logansport, Indiana.

WITH PISTOL AND AXE
Two Lives Are Taken in a Terrible Family Tragedy.

BLOOMINGTON, Ind., Sept. 8-At 1 o'clock in the morning Dale Judah went to the home of his father-in-law, Richard Wright, at Payne, ten miles from here, and called the old man out. When Wright passed through the doorway, Judah fired at him with a pistol, but the shot did not take effect. The two men grappled, and during the struggle Wright called for his youngest daughter to knock Judah off with an axe. Judah fired three shots into the old man's body, and just as he shot the last time, the daughter struck him with a terrible blow on the back of the head with an axe, killing him instantly. Wright also died in a few minutes. Judah had some trouble with his wife and supposed that she had gone to her father's house. He got drunk and went there, intent upon the killing the old man and his wife, but she was not at the place, having concluded to stay with a neighbor.

The Lowell Daily Sun, September 8, 1892.
Lowell, Massachusetts.

Despite the lack of a definitive motive behind the shooting reported in the next story, it is reasonable to assume its origin

53

stemmed from a domestic dispute between the involved parties.

SHOOTING AFFAIR AT VERONA

A shooting affair occurred on Thursday afternoon of last week at Verona, between Ramsay and Wakefield, as a result of which Mr. and Mrs. Domenic Coco are in the county jail on a charge of murderous assault and Sabatori Dorsey lies at the Wakefield hospital suffering from three serious bullet wounds, and the attending physicians say that he cannot possibly recover.

None of the parties connected with the affair have given any reason for the shooting, Dorsey claiming that he doesn't know, and the Coco's refusing to say anything about the trouble.

The Coco's keep a boarding house and Dorsey boarded with them. They are all Italians. Last Thursday afternoon Dorsey was shot by either Mr. or Mrs. Coco, the weapon used being a .22 calibre automatic revolver. The aim of the marksman was very true, one of the bullets entering Dorsey's head just in front of his right ear, the second entering his body a couple inches in front of the right shoulder and the third penetrating his right side about six inches above the hip. This latter bullet passed completely through his body and penetrated the lungs; the first bullet which entered near his right temple, the doctors say, is lodged in the back of his head.

Dorsey, in a death-bed statement made by him, said that Coco fired the first shot and then handed the gun over to his wife who fired the other two, but Mrs. Coco says that this is not true, claiming that she fired all three shots. The officers say also that there are many witnesses who will testify that Coco was at work at the mine when the shooting occurred and therefore couldn't have fired any of the shots.

Dorsey is a single man about 24 years of age, and the Coco's are also comparatively young people.

Attorney J. A. O'Neill of this city has been retained by the defense.

The Ironwood Times, December 14, 1918.
Ironwood, Michigan.

Political races can generate a great deal of animosity between candidates vying for the same office. While most politicians manage to contain their anger there has been examples in which these tensions can reach the boiling point, thus leading to violence. In the following account, two politicians attempt to settle their differences in a general store.

Criminal Calendar

John Ambler Smith and George D. Wise, republican and democratic candidates for congress from the Richmond district, met at McKinney's store in Caroline county. Wise threw a tumbler at Smith. The latter drew his revolver, when Wise beat a retreat behind a dry goods box. Smith was arrested.

Freeborn Co. Standard, November 9, 1882.
Alberta Lea, Minnesota.

In line with the preceding tale of politicians behaving badly is the following account of a riot erupting at a political convention being held in the Indian Territory, which became the state of Oklahoma later that year.

CONVENTION IN RIOT

Muskogee I. T. July 18-An attempt by Henry Asp, a railroad attorney of Guthrie, to address the Republican county convention here today converted the meeting into a howling, fighting mob.

Pistols were brandished, knives were flashed and chairs were wielded right and left, resulting in bruises and minor injuries to several persons. Officers with drawn pistols, who threatened to shoot into the crowd if the fighting did not stop, failed to quell the disturbance. United States Deputy Marshal Bud Ledbetter appeared on the scene and practically took charge of the meeting. Ledbetter, who is a Democrat, saved Asp from being mobbed, and prevented bloodshed. Asp, pale and trembling, was taken away from the meeting. The trouble started when the anti-Franz and anti-statehood forces, of which

Asp is a member, attempted to address the meeting before the organization was perfected. The Franz forces were victorious in the test vote for temporary chairman, and the other element then subsided and quiet was restored.

The Salt Lake Tribune, July 19, 1907.
Salt Lake City, Utah.

The following pair of accounts prove that women are equally adept as men in orchestrating criminal acts.

WOMAN HELD AS ROBBER LEADER

Chicago, December 27-Miss Elizabeth Baker, a handsome woman, dressed in the height of fashion, was being held today by the police as the leader of a band of eight men who have accumulated more than $6,000 worth of stolen property in the last few days. Miss Baker was taken on a charge of receiving stolen property, and the detectives who raided her apartments on the north side said they found evidence that the woman was the directing spirit of the robber band. The eight alleged robbers were arrested also. Confessions, the detectives said, were obtained from two of the men indicating that Miss Baker planned their raids and directed the manner in which the homes of the wealthy persons were to be robbed of their jewelry.

Logansport Pharos-Reporter, December 27, 1913.
Logansport, Indiana.

Woman Holds Up Cafe.

ST. LOUIS, Dec. 31.-A young woman garbed as a man entered a restaurant here early today levelled a revolver at Monroe White, proprietor and ordered him to hand over the contents of the cash drawer or get "plugged." White complied giving her $27. He said he recognized her as a woman by her voice features and part of her hair which was visible under her cap.

Joplin News Herald, January 1, 1922.
Joplin, Missouri.

Not all robbery victims are easily parted from their valuables. In instances such as these, a little more persuasion may be required as the robber of Professor Connelley discovered.

"OH, GO AWAY" SAID A PROFESSOR TO ROBBER

Chicago, July 21.-Prof. Clifford B. Connelley, dean of the School of Applied Industries at the Carnegie Institute, Pittsburg, who passed through Chicago last night, contributed $230 and a diamond ring to the highwaymen who held up the North Coast Limited Thursday night near Buffalo, N. D.

When a masked man thrust a revolver between Pullman berth curtains and ordered Prof. Connelley to "Hand over all he had or get shot," the professor pushed back the hand that held the weapon and said: "Oh, go away and quit your fooling."

It wasn't until another hand came through the curtains and wrenched a diamond ring from his finger almost taking the finger with it, that the professor fully awakened. The he sat up and placed in the unarmed hand $230.

The Portsmouth Daily Times, July 21, 1911.
Portsmouth, Ohio.

As demonstrated by the next three accounts, the circumstances leading up to some criminal acts are beyond the realm of common sense.

Killed Over a Game of Dominoes.

Scranton, Pa., Nov 6.-Quarrelling over a game of dominoes in a North Scranton saloon Thursday night, John Orgill, formerly constable of the First ward, plunged a knife into the abdomen of Robert Eliott. The latter fell dying to the floor, while Orgill stood over him, amazed at his act. Elliot died yesterday. Orgillis [sic] 67 years old, and his victim was 51. Both men are married and have families. Orgill is in jail.

The News, November 6, 1897.
Frederick, Maryland.

A CHICAGO INCIDENT.
Man Killed Over a Dispute About 50 Cents
Slayer Saved From Mob.

Chicago, Ill., June 15.-Two men fought for the possession of 50 cents, and when the struggle ended one was dead and the other on his knees, pleading with an infuriated mob to spare his life. The timely arrival of the police prevented a lynching. John Czech and Kazmir Kochanski had a disagreement over the value of a piece of old copper that one had bought from the other. Angry words led to blows. During the fight Czech picked up the bent and battered barrel of a rifle. He whirled the weapon about his head, bringing it down on his adversary's skull with such force that Kochanski fell dead. Then the mob flocked about the two men. Czech was seized hold by a dozen men. Everybody wanted to drag him to a lamp post and lynch him, and were only prevented by the arrival of the police, who found the man on his knees begging for mercy.

The Galveston Daily News, June 16, 1901.
Galveston, Texas.

Flattened Pancake.

St. Louis, Oct. 18.-Mrs. Annie Lachs, the woman who threw the pancake into Mrs. Cleveland's lap when the presidential party were at the fair grounds in this city, was fined $50 in the police court today. The woman disclaimed any disrespect for Mrs. Cleveland, and she said she threw it in a spirit of fun; but the testimony was against her, and the court thought the fun worth $50. The woman took an appeal.

The Daily Huronite, October 19, 1887.
Huron, Dakota Territory (South Dakota).

The following example relates how the perpetrator of a relatively minor infraction was fortunate the police arrived in time to rescue him from a group of enraged citizens.

A HUGGER IN TROUBLE.

Norfolk, Va., April 22-L. B. Plummer, a well known young man, narrowly escaped a lynching at the hands of infuriated citizens after hugging a prominent young woman on the street.

Plummer had followed the girl for several blocks when he threw his arms suddenly around her and gave her a good hug. The girl screamed and the man was given a good thrashing by several men who happened to be in the neighborhood.

A crowd gathered, but an officer succeeded in rescuing the man from them. The name of the young woman was suppressed by the police.

Semi Weekly Waterloo Courier, April 23, 1907.

Waterloo, Iowa.

In the next tale, four enterprising turkey thieves make the mistake of leaving a trail leading directly to where they intended to prepare their stolen birds for the oven. Regardless of being caught red-handed, the four perpetrators of this petty criminal act nonetheless managed to easily escape the long arm of the law.

STOLEN TURKEYS FOUND IN OVEN
RESTAURANTEUR MISSES BIRDS;
STARTS SEARCH; FINDS THEM
IN THE PALM.

When J. Curley, proprietor of the lunch counter in the Kern Hotel building appeared at his place of business yesterday morning he found two turkeys missing. A line of turkey feathers beginning at Curley's place and leading up to the back door of the Palm saloon led Curley to get out a search warrant. Marshal Badger and Constable Stroble searched for the missing turkeys.

The proprietor, when questioned said he had given permission to some men to use his kitchen to do cooking and that the officers might investigate. Four men were engaged in preparing a fine big turkey for the oven. While the officers were searching for the other missing turkey the men made their escape.

The Bakersfield Californian, December 9, 1909.
Bakersfield, California.

Some twenty-seven years prior to the above-mentioned turkey theft incidents, a quarrel over the same creatures led to the shooting death described by the following article.

CRIMINAL CALENDAR.

Bart Scully was instantly killed at Paris, Ky., by Hooker Stivers. The parties lived on adjoining farms and the women became engaged in a quarrel about turkeys. Sherman Stivers seventeen years old, brother of Hooker Stivers took a shot gun and shot the turkeys claimed by Sculley's housekeeper. Scully returned from Memphis races, and hearing of the case, and meeting young Stivers in a spring wagon, took him out and boxed his ears. When Hooker Stivers heard of this he put a shotgun in his buggy and came to town to meet Scully, calling him (Scully) towards him. When Scully got within a few feet, Stivers deliberately shot him dead.

Freeborn Co. Standard, November 9, 1882.
Alberta Lea, Minnesota.

Over the years, burglars have discovered ingenious methods of perpetrating their crimes, an example of which is in the following excerpt.

Neat Trick of Burglars.

NEW ORLEANS, Nov. 17.-Burglars sawed a hole from the floor above and with a rope for a ladder carried away $5,000 worth of old coins from J. J. Bettro's office.

The Evening Herald, November 18, 1893.
Oskaloosa, Iowa.

The term miser describes a person with the compulsion to

hoard money while possessing an innate fear of losing it. One can only imagine the mental anguish experienced by the person in following story suffering from this affliction.

POLICE CAPTURE GANG OF THIEVES

New Milford, Conn., April 8-By the capture and confession of Andrew Turner, aged 17, of Lanesville, the police this morning were enabled to capture a gang of five youths who robbed Henry Davis, a miser, of twelve thousand dollars at Turner's home in Lanesville Thursday. Turner saw Davis counting his money and planned the robbery. His four companions were arrested at Waterbury this morning and ten thousand dollars was recovered.

Cedar Rapids Sunday Republican, April 10, 1904.
Cedar Rapids, Iowa.

On the morning of April 18, 1906, San Francisco suffered a major earthquake, which, along with the resulting fire, killed over 3,000 people. Besides those killed, over 225,000 of the city's inhabitants found themselves homeless, one of which, with the assistance of his aunt, took advantage of his uncle's generosity. The result is this rather lengthy account appearing nearly a month and half following the disaster.

REFUGEE STEAL CLOTHES OF HIS BENEFACTOR, THEN ELOPES WITH HIS WIFE!

A refugee who stole his benefactor's clothes and wife, was arrested here this morning by Sheriff Frank Barnet on a warrant from Los Angeles, and the man is now in custody awaiting the arrival of officers from the southern county. His companion made her escape.

The man in the case is George Christ, who, also at times, takes the name of Stokes. He is 29 years of age and was burned out of his haunts in San Francisco and in response to an

61

invitation went to Los Angeles where he was provided with all he needed by his uncle and aunt, Mr. and Mrs. F. Naegele.

SHE IS GOOD LOOKING.

While well preserved and a good looking woman, Mrs. Alvina Naegele is described as at least ten years her companion's senior, but this did not prevent her taking such a liking to him, that she agreed to leave her husband for her nephew. To do this they pawned a piano and sold some of the most valuable household effects belonging to her husband, and with the proceeds quietly took the train and left for parts unknown. Naegele's wrath was unbounded when he discovered their perfidy and he immediately swore to a warrant charging them with the theft of his goods. Sheriff White of Los Angeles came north with the warrant and the husband and they spent several days in the city and San Francisco trying to locate the pair but without success.

GAVE NOTICE.

General notice was sent out by Sheriff Frank Barnet and Marshal Carey of Emeryville said that he knew Christ, and this morning met him on the Broadway and took him into custody. He was taken to the sheriff's office and later to the county jail. When asked where he had been staying he said that he was living at the Merritt Hotel with his wife, and without losing any more time Sheriff Barnet sent a deputy there to take the woman into custody. But the bird had already flown. The woman, he was informed, had ordered her trunks taken to the Sixteenth street station last night and stated that she was going to Los Angeles on the Owl.

MAKES CONFESSION.

Christ or Stokes does not deny coming north with the woman, but denies that he stole anything and said the he only acted as Mrs. Naegele's agent in securing a loan on the piano and other goods, and said the he supposed they belonged to her. The piano, Naegele said, was the property of a niece of Mrs. Naegele. They secured $100 on the piano and about as much more on other things they pawned and sold.

Sheriff Barnet was very much disappointed to think he lost the man's companion, but he believe that she will be arrested at the other end of the line and already has sent telegrams to Los Angeles to give the officers there notice of her coming. The pair had been at the Merritt Hotel since last Tuesday.

Oakland Tribune, June 1, 1906.
Oakland, California.

In the following narrative, we remain in San Francisco to learn that not even the specter of an impending disaster will deter some enterprising criminals from seizing any opportunity to conduct their nefarious business.

ROBBED DURING A PANIC

SAN FRANCISCO, June 1.-John Lambke, a passenger on the steamer Santa Barbara, which broke down while coming into port, is minus $150 as a result of the accident, and A. L. Croton, a fellow passenger, is under arrest on suspicion of having taken the money.

The panic which followed the break down caused those on board to forget to take the ordinary precaution of protecting their belongings.

The arrested man is alleged to have taken possession of Lambke's money during the excitement. He denies that he stole the money. When searched the found $115 on Croton.

Oakland Tribune, June 1, 1906.
Oakland, California.

The growth of the United States during the eighteenth century fueled the expansion of the railroads. As these companies transported large amounts of valuable goods, they quickly became popular targets for thievery and robbery. Of note in the following story, is that the value of the stolen property amounts to between $840 thousand and $1.1 million in today's money.

CHICAGO special: James O'Malley, who it is said, has robbed various railroads of thousands of dollars, was arrested in this city. O'Malley was employed as a conducter on the Minneapolis, St. Paul and Sault Ste. Marie railroad, and for nearly five years is believed to have been the leader of a gang which systematically robbed the cars of the company. It is estimated that the company was robbed during that time of property worth between $30,000 and $40,000. Detectives succeeded in arresting and convicting all the thieves with the exception of O'Malley.

The Gazette, September 13, 1895.
Cedar Falls, Iowa.

Reports of corruption in city government appear quite regularly in the media. The next article, however, provides proof that such dishonest proceedings are nothing new.

BUTTE, Mont., special: Warrants have been issued for the arrest of ex-City Clerk Irvine and his assistant, Phillip Miller, and a number of other ex-city officials, on the charge of forgery committed during their terms in office. It is alleged they issued warrants to fictitious persons in sums believed to aggregate $25,000. The accused are believed to have left town. It is believed that if they are arrested they will make disclosures involving many persons high in the business and social circles here.

The Gazette, September 13, 1895.
Cedar Falls, Iowa.

A person's unique talent usually becomes apparent at a young age. In keeping with this theme, the following account relates a young man's inherent skills of forgery.

FORGERY CASE AGAINST BOY

SPENCERVILLE-(Special)-So clever was Donald Wycuff, 12-year old boy, a student of the seventh grade of the Spencerville schools, with a pen, that he was able to forge checks that even fooled the cashier at one of the local banks.

The lad, taken from the Allen-co Children's Home was living with Mr. and Mrs. Melvin Shillinger. Finding a check book, the property of John Davies, he forged three checks, it is charged. One for $20; one for $9.73, and the third for $17.00. Two of the checks he cashed in person at the bank, officers say. When taken into custody he confessed and was turned over to the proper authorities at Lima.

The Lima News, February 9, 1921.
Lima, Ohio.

Concerning a brazen robbery carried out by two army soldiers during the winter of 1923, the next narrative could have just as easily been the plot for a television program or motion picture.

LIFE WAS TOO TAME FOR ARMY CORPORALS

Newport News, Va., Jan. 31.-Military authorities at Langley filed announced late today that Coporals J. S. Wood and James Harvey of the 58th service squadron, will be tried by a military court on charges of robbing the post's pay car of $43,000 following the sensational kidnapping of the finance officer and his guard of four enlisted men in Hampton yesterday.

The announcement was made following a lengthy investigation of the robbery by a board of inquiry appointed by the post commandant, and after Wood and Harvey were said to have confessed the robbery and detailed its execution for the benefit of the board. The men did not implicate a third party in the hold-up, it was said, although the victims of the kidnapping and robbery declared the two bandits referred to a man they called "Smitty" frequently during the ride over the peninsula. Officers are still investigating this phase of the case and they are looking for a woman with whom, it is said, one of the corporals was intimate.

"Life was not worth living the way things were going with us and we decided to get some money have one real fling or get killed in the attempt," the corporals were quoted as saying when questioned by the Langley field officials today. The officers said this was the only motive the men gave for the robbery.

Wood and Harvey volunteered to take the officers over the route they traveled through the woods after abandoning the government car near Big Bethel yesterday in an effort to find the $2,789.94 which they said they lost while dodging searching parties. The men were said to have expressed the belief that they lost the money when they emptied the leather bag in which Capt. Norman D. Cota carried the pay roll. This money had not been recovered early tonight, although authorities at Langley field stated the remainder of the $43,000 seized in the robbery was recovered when the two men were arrested by a posse near Hampton last night.

Burlington Daily News, February 1, 1923.
Burlington, North Carolina.

In the following case, the citizens of a small town in the Indian Territory (later part of the state of Oklahoma) take matters into their own hands in an attempt to thwart a group of bank robbers assaulting a local bank.

LOOT KIOWA BANK.

South McAlester, I. T., Dec. 28.-A gang of five robbers looted the bank at Kiowa at 3 a. m. and escaped after several hundred shots had been exchanged between the robbers and a posse of fifty citizens of Kiowa.

The robbers dynamited the safe and secured $2,800 in cash, some of which is believed to have been mutilated by the explosion. The bank building was partially wrecked.

An entrance to the bank was gained by the use of crowbars through a rear window. While two of the men did the work of blowing the safe, three remained outside as guards. The first explosion was a failure, making a loud report, but doing little damage. The citizens heard the report and, arming themselves with revolvers and shotguns, a volley was fired at the robbers inside, who were visible through the shutters. The fire was returned by the guards secreted on the outside. While the two men on the inside worked, the three men on the outside kept up a steady fire with the posse of citizens. It took three explosions to open the safe. After the last explosion the burglars gathered up the money, and leaving through the front of the bank, got away in the darkness.

Semi-Weekly Telegraph, January 1, 1904.
Atlantic, Iowa.

In modern times, one of the first steps following a person's arrest is to have their picture taken at the police station. While this is a common practice today the world over, this was not always the case.

ARRESTED THREE TIMES, YOU'RE PICTURE TAKEN

Asuncion, July 3-Persons arrested for drunkeness more than three times a year in Paraguay will be considered confirmed drunkards and their photographs posted in saloons and police stations under the provisions of a bill which has been approved by the senate and is now before the lower house.

The law would also forbid the sale of liquor in theaters, moving picture houses, race tracks and other places of public gathering and within two hundred meters of places where laborers work. The president is empowered to issue a decree determining the alcoholic content of intoxicating liquors and fixing other restrictions tending to make their consumption less injurious to the public health. Provision is also made for anti-alcoholic propaganda in the public schools.

The Bismarck Tribune, July 3, 1920.
Bismarck, North Dakota.

Sometimes a release from jail is only a temporary reprieve, as discovered by this bartender in 1899.

OBTAINS HIS LIBERTY TO BE REARRESTED.

Chicago, Dec. 24.-William H. Armstrong, bartender for "Big Dan" Coughlin, and who, with his employer, was indicted for conspiracy in the noted Carbine-Illinois Central bribery case last July, has just obtained his freedom in Seattle through a decision rendered by the Supreme Court of the State of Washington. The court held that the complaint did not set forth facts sufficient to constitute a crime.

State's Attorney Deneon telegraphed to Detective Tyrrell, who has been in Seattle ever since Armstrong was arrested, to have the fugitive and the woman with whom he fled from Chicago arrested on a charge of living together unlawfully.

The Post Standard, December 25, 1899.

Syracuse, New York.

As the next tale relates, not everyone that has committed an infraction of the law is unwilling to repent by making a voluntary restitution.

REPENTED FOURFOLD.

Iowa Falls, Ia., Aug. 31.-Defrauding a weighing machine of 1 cent and returning fourfold, a Waterloo man, conscience stricken, seeks to settle on the gospel plan and make proper restitution. The agent of the Rock Island road at Clarion is in receipt of a letter containing 4 cents in postage cents. The accompanying note indicates the moral regeneration of the sender who mailed the latter at Waterloo:

"A short time since I defrauded the weighing machine in your station of 1 cent. This was wrong. The writer returns it fourfold-the bible plan."

The O'Brien County Bell, August 31, 1905.

Primghar, Iowa.

In today's world, the term bootleg usually refers to the illegal reproduction of video or sound productions. In the traditional sense, however, it popularly defined the illegal production and distribution of alcohol. In the following excerpt, we see how some moonshiners attempted to turn the tables on a law officer.

Bootleggers "Arrest" Officer of Law

HUNTINGTON, W. Va., July 24.-Seized by a gang of alleged moonshiners, brought before a Green Brier county justice of the peace and found guilty of on a charge of bootlegging was the experience of H. R. Ratliff, of Hinton, W. Va., a state prohibition officer who returned from an investigation tour into the hills. Ratliff was sentenced to serve sixty days in jail by the justice, but was rescued by Harry Fitzgerald, a brother officer, from an alleged moonshiner, who was escorting the convicted official to the bastile [sic].

Ratliff and Fitzgerald went into the hills of Green Brier to investigate a report that many illicit stills were in operation there. The officers located two stills and Ratliff went to the village of Auto, W. Va., to telephone the department at Charleston for additional men to make the raid. While in Auto Ratliff was arrested by the gang of alleged moonshiners at the point of revolvers and brought before the justice, charged with bootlegging, and was convicted.

Following the rescue of Ratliff by Fitzgerald the officers destroyed two stills and more than six thousand gallons of mash and swore out 19 warrants for Green Brier county residents, who are charged with manufacturing moonshine.

The Daily Republican-News, July 24, 1919.
Hamilton, Ohio.

Riots are one of the most dreaded scenarios that anyone employed in law enforcement must be prepared to confront. While the causes of such outbreaks of violence vary, the next four episodes of this form of lawlessness revolve around the subject of religion.

POLISH PRIEST ASSAULTED.

MANISTEE, Mich., May 4.-A Polish priest was assaulted on the street this morning by one faction of his church. A general riot resulted, in which men and women participated. The militia were called out to quell the riot. The fire department

69

was also called out and turned their hose upon the mob. After nearly drowning several of the rioters, peace was restored. The sheriff attempted to arrest the leaders, and was attacked by women, several of whom were knocked down. Ten rioters have been jailed. A guard has been stationed at the priest's house to prevent further trouble.

The trouble commenced three months ago over money matters. The people to the number of one-third of the congregation were opposed to Rev. Father Grochowski, whom they claimed has compelled them to pay exorbitant taxes to support the church. Six of the ring-leaders were arrested for assault and battery in February, but after a trial were acquitted. Since that time the trouble has continued; two parties running the Church; both selling pews and transacting the business. Last Sunday the priest went through the church asking for the certificates of pew-holders. Purlel, one of his opponents, drew a knife and told the priest the knife was his certificate. A riot ensued. Yesterday women attacked the priest and his factions. The police dispersed the crowd, but the trouble was renewed this morning. Trouble is expected to-morrow.

The Salt Lake Daily Tribune, May 5, 1889.
Salt Lake City, Utah.

MOB BURNS "HOLLY ROLLER" CHURCH

Newton Feb 19-The burning of the Springs Holiness church, the wholesale arrest of its members and the conviction of five more persons were yesterday's developments in the court action and mob action against a religious band known as "Holy Rollers" near here.

The trial is the outgrowth of a special service at the Springs church a week ago, at which it is alleged two little boys were tied hand and foot and after a vote of the congregation were beaten with sticks and leather straps until their backs bled. The "Rollers' it is charged took this means of driving the "sin and devil" out of the boys. The little fellows, nine and twelve years old on the witness stand said the sin with which they were charged was failure to attend church regularly.

The church of the recently organized sect was found burned to the ground early this morning. It is presumed the mob which yesterday was frustrated in its efforts to lynch the pastor of the church and three others charged with the attack on the boys is responsible for the fire.

Mrs. Rosa Deck[,] Frank Emery and his wife, Allen Lyons[,] and Harold Cummins were today found guilty of being accessories to the attack on the boys. Each of the first three were fined $85 and costs and the two latter $65 and costs each.

Feeling[s] against the new sect and determination to rid the community of all its believers was expressed openly during the trials.

The Daily Review, February 19, 1914.
Decatur, Illinois.

CHURCH RIOT QUELLED BY STATE TROOPERS AT BUTLER

BUTLER, Pa., May 3.-Five persons were injured, one probably fatally, and 13 others are under arrest as the result of a riot today between Roman Catholics and Greek Catholics of Butler township. There has been bitter feeling [sic] between the two religious bodies for several weeks.

The Butler troop of the Pennsylvania state constabulary was rushed to the scene and quickly quelled the disturbance. Further trouble is feared and the state troopers will remain in the district for the present.

The Morning Herald, May 4, 1914.
Uniontown, Pennsylvania.

PARTICIPANT IN RECENT SOUTH BEND CHURCH RIOT SAID TO BE INSANE.

SOUTH BEND, Ind., Sept. 22-Louis Grajozyk, a west side resident, believed to be insane, is in a serious condition as a result of having jumped from the second story window in the house of Rev. Stanilaus Gruza, pastor of the St. Casimir's Polish

.Catholic church. Father Gruza was recently the center of a church riot on the west side in which a number of people were injured. Grajozyk was in the riot. He is since said to have gone insane. He appeared at the home of the priest, declaring he would kill him, according to the father's story, and leaped from the window when the Rev. Mr. Gruza called the authorities.

Fort Wayne Journal-Gazette, September 23, 1914.

Fort Wayne, Indiana.

In the next account, a police officer traveling on a train attempts to intervene during a fight only to find himself confronted by an angry mob. Subsequent events quickly got out of hand and led to deadly consequences for both him and a pair of the rioters.

ROW ON A TRAIN.

CUMBERLAND, Md., July 28.-Sunday an excursion train from Johnstown, Pa., brought about 1,200 people to this city on a pleasure trip. They left Sunday night at 6:30 on the return trip. When near Rockwood, Pa., a fight took place between some drunken men on the platform of one of the cars, to quell which, James Kelly, a policeman from Johnstown, drew a revolver. This action angered the crowd and they made a rush for him between the cars while the train was running at a rate of forty miles an hour.

The conductor signalled the train to stop, the coupling broke and Kelly dropped under the wheels and was crushed to death. Lucius Meyers, of Latrobe, was thrown from the platform under the wheels and killed. Milton Pyle, of Somerset, was thrown against some rocks in the ditch and had his skull fractured and a broken leg, from the effects of which he died soon after arriving in Somerset.

Hamilton Daily Democrat, July 28, 1891.

Hamilton, Ohio.

As one of the principal characters in the next anecdote discovered, the life of an outlaw is fraught with hidden, and sometimes fatal, dangers.

STRUCK THE WRONG GIRL.

Seventeen miles below Fayetteville, N. C., Albert Gilmore, a notorious outlaw from South Carolina, entered the house of the Rev. William Brunt yesterday, and finding no one but Miss Brunt there, forced her to prepare dinner for him at the point of a pistol. After eating heartily, with an oath he leaped out the window. Miss Brunt grabbed a gun and fired 13 buckshot, striking Gilmore, from which he died in a few minutes. A reward of $300 was out for Gilmore, to which Miss Burnt becomes entitled, and she is the hero of the hour.

Indiana Progress, May 25, 1892.

Indiana, Pennsylvania.

There is an old saying that you cannot take it with you, and in the next story, we will witness grave robbers attempting to prove the truth of this adage. The length of this article indicates that Mlle Lantelme's popularity on the French stage during this timeframe had spread to America. An interesting point in the following account is that the perpetrators of the crime came within a hair's breadth of achieving their villainous goal, only to come away with nothing.

GHOULS OPEN VAULT

Paris.-Mlle. Lantelme, the lovely actress who was cut off in the flower of her youth and beauty, was not allowed to rest quietly even in her grave. Ghouls recently broke into her tomb to steal the jewels which were buried with her and left the broken coffin beneath clouds of smoke.

The outrage was perpetrated at the great Paris cemetery of Pere la Chaise. The thieves were unable to find the jewels, which had been placed in a small sack beneath the dead beauty's head, and were found untouched by authorities. The

73

jewels are two large pearls, a pearl necklace and a pendant consisting of a large pear shaped black pearl and emeralds, of a total value of about $10,000.

Mlle. Lantelme, one of the most beautiful and most promising actresses of the French stage, was married to M. Alfred Edwards, one of the founders of the Le Matin, and a prominent figure in Parisian life. She was drowned in the Rhine last July while taking a holiday on board a kind of houseboat yacht, L'Aimee, with a number of friends. After retiring to rest one hot evening she fell from the wide open windows of the houseboat into the swift current and was drowned. Her body was drawn up from the river clad in evening dress and many jewels.

The news of her death caused a deep impression as she was famous for her beauty, her marvelous jewels and toilettes and her ready wit.

The body was brought to Paris for burial in the Edwards family vault at Pere la Chaise, and her husband insisted that her favorite jewels should be interned with her. This was done, and the fact evidently excited the cupidity of the authors of the outrage.

The violation of the vault was discovered by a cemetery attendant, who, when passing the Edwards chapel, noticed that a stained-glass window had been smashed. The door of the little chapel was open and the interior was full of smoke. The attendant immediately gave the alarm, and the local police inspector with a number of constables arrived.

The police discovered that the thieves had entered by means of a small stained-glass window about three feet high at the back of the altar. The thieves moved the stout iron bars, protecting the window on the outside and broke the thick glass. One of them must have cut himself, for blood stains were found everywhere inside and outside the vault and along the route pursued by the robbers to the cemetery wall, over which they climbed.

In order to have more room to work the thieves handed out

from the chapel the handsome Byzantine cross which stood on the altar and a number of vases and other objects. Having gained the floor of the chapel the thieves raised three great flagstones concealing the vault and thus exposed the leaden coffin containing the actress' remains. Cutting through the shell they unscrewed the lid.

They then laid bare the body, which was surrounded by lint. Finding that the jewels were not round the neck of the corpse they abandoned their search. It is possible that the wounded thief was overcome by the atmosphere of the place and that his accomplice or accomplices had to get him away before they were discovered.

The police found cotton wool all about the floor. It was smoldering, the thieves having apparently dropped a match by accident, and the chapel was full of smoke. Firemen were sent for before further investigations were made, for the impure air and smoke rising from the vault rendered further action impossible.

The Edwards vault is a narrow little chapel in gray stone with an inscription over the door running "Famille Edwards, Requies Aeterna." It stands in a broad avenue of cypresses in the new part of the cemetery.

Atlantic News-Telegraph, January 30, 1912.
Atlantic, Iowa.

The practice of tarring and feathering was a common component of mob justice in American culture during the eighteenth and nineteenth centuries. Over time, this method of punishment became less popular, but isolated incidents of this practice were still being reported well into the 1900s.

Tarred and Feathered in New York.

NEW YORK, Oct. 11.-A man named William Pryor was found tarred and feathered in the streets of Brooklyn early in the morning. The man was partially undressed, his shirt being torn off, so that his body from the waist to the shoulder was exposed. The portion of the body exposed to view was covered with a thick layer of tar which had been liberally sprinkled with feathers. He had been chloroformed. When he recovered consciousness he said he had been assaulted by two unknown men. Their reason for the deed is a mystery.

The Sunday Republican, October 12, 1890.

Mitchell, South Dakota.

TARRED, FEATHERED AND RIDDEN ON RAIL IS CLEM SMITH'S FATE

Findlay, July 19-At Van Buren, north of here, Clem N. Smith, accused of mistreating small boys, was last night tarred, feathered and ridden on a rail, then driven out of town and hanged in effigy. Only the advice of cooler heads prevented a lynching. Nearly every man in the village was a member of the mob. The town marshall [sic] said he was sick and went home before the mob started to work.

The Newark Advocate, July 19, 1907.

Newark, Ohio.

Although it will be forever unknown if the meals made with the chickens stolen by the man in the next story were delicious, it is beyond doubt of their expensiveness as the fines imposed upon him were equivalent to over $1,200 in today's money. Besides the financial penalty, the punishment imposed by the Judge also included a month in jail and a temporary suspension of voting privileges. All of which adds up to some expensive chicken dinners.

PAID A HIGH PRICE FOR A FEW CHICKENS

Last week Samuel Bush paid dearly for some chickens he got last fall without asking the price of the owner. It was an inconvenient hour of the day to call up the owner, Geo. M. Robbins, and ask him the price, so Mr. Bush just "took them along." Robbins found it out and told the grand jury, and it became a serious matter. The case has been on the docket since last fall, and last week the case came up again, and Mr. Bush came from Paris, Ill., where he had moved in the meantime. He admitted that he got the chickens, and it remained for the judge to set the price, and the price he set showed that he did not approve of Mr. Bush's way of getting chickens. The price was a $20.00 fine, $26.00 in costs, 30 days in jail and disfranchisement for six years.

The Sullivan Democrat, June 9, 1904.
Sullivan, Indiana.

In this chapter's final account, we read of a young man with a terrible affliction, for which a judge in Kansas City, Missouri believes he has found a remedy.

IN CELL TO ESCAPE WOMEN.

Kansas City, Mo., Oct 9.-"We will protect you from the women for a while." Judge Carlisle of the municipal court, told a dashing young iron molder. "I do not think they will follow you to the workhouse. One hundred days."

The sentence followed the youth's arrest for lighting with a boarding house keeper. His defense was that in every place he stayed his landlady's daughters fell in love with him.

The Weekly Sentinel, October 23, 1912.
Fort Wayne, Indiana.

Chapter Five
Judicial and Law Enforcement Predicaments

In a process that has continued over the centuries, our civilization has created a complex legal system to address criminal acts and settle disputes. While the preceding chapter dealt with the actual criminal acts themselves, this section will relate tales involving the enforcement of the law and a variety of other legal matters such as civil proceedings.

One method utilized in the fight to prevent individuals from becoming hardened criminals is aggressively punishing unlawfulness attitudes at a young age. In this section's first example, we witness how a judge took a unique approach in handling an infraction committed by a youth.

JUDGE DECIDES TO DO SPANKING

Utica, N.Y., November 12-City Judge O'Connor has reached the determination that hereafter all juvenile first offenders who are brought before him shall be spanked and the judge himself will administer the punishment. The first victim, a ten-year-old boy, charged with petit larceny, was before the court today.

"I want him sent up," said the lad's father. The man said that he could not control the boy and could not make him go to school.

"A man who publicly admits he can't control his child is not fit to be a father," said the court.

Judge O'Conner then turned to the lad and called him to the bench. Securing a good sized wooden paddle, the court laid the lad across his lap and administered several raps in the good old-fashioned manner.

"Now, go home and go to school and don't you dare skip or steal. If you do, I'll come down and give you a lacing as you

never got at home," said the court, as he allowed the youngster
to wriggle from his lap.

Logansport Pharos-Reporter, November 12, 1913.
Logansport, Indiana.

Serving on a jury can be an extremely demanding experience
for certain individuals. As the following story relates, the
emotional stress of a trial can push some jurors past their limits
of self-control.

JUROR NOW A MANIAC

Cambridge, Mass., May 10. The development of insanity by
Willis A. White of Maynard, one of the jurors who on May 4
convicted Chester S. Jordan of the murder of his wife, will be
used by Jordan's attorneys in their plea for a new trial.

White returned home at Maynard Tuesday, showing marked
effects of the strain of the trial, and yesterday he was sent to the
Worcester insane hospital.

White was taken to Concord in an automobile from Maynard,
and during a brief stop in front of the District Court building he
became violent and implored the spectators who gathered
about the machine either to save him or shoot him. In the
courtroom it was found necessary to administer a hypodermic
injection to quiet him. White is a tall, strong farmer and it was
difficult to overpower him.

Allegany County Reporter, May 11, 1909.
Wellsville, New York.

Today, it is common practice for elected officials to make
decisions concerning their own pay raises. According to the
following excerpt, however, it appears that such a practice has, at
times, been frowned upon.

PETER GUILTY.

By Associated Press.

Des Moines, Oct. 11-By a decision of the Iowa supreme court
today Peter Olinger, mayor of Dubuque in 1895, was adjudged

liable for prosecution because he engaged in raising his salary from $1,500 to $2,000. The case is similar to the action against the aldermen, similarly decided Friday.

The Waterloo Courier, October 13, 1897.
Waterloo, Iowa.

A career in law enforcement is strewn with many obstacles, some of which are obvious, while others are not.

TALKED TOO MUCH.
A Frisco Police Captain In Trouble for
Telling the Truth.

San Francisco, April 19.-Charges have been filed with the police commissioners against Police Captain Mooney by Chief Dinan, who says that on April 12 Captain Mooney stated that to his positive knowledge the police commissioners as they at present stand were appointed for a purpose; that the department is reeking with corruption and that in his own company he knew that fully half of his men were corrupt. The rules of the police department forbid any police officer making strictures on any member of the department until the charges are passed upon by the police commissioners.

Semi Weekly Waterloo Courier, April 23, 1907.
Waterloo, Iowa.

Wouldn't Wear Brass Buttons So He's Fired

Because Desk Sergeant Ed Bailey of the night police force refused to observe a recent order of Chief of Police Depew and wear a uniform, he has lost his desk job, for the time being at least, and John S. Barger acted as desk sergeant last night.

"All captains and sergeants must be in uniform," said the chief. "This joint is beginning to look like a country precinct. If a man comes in to make a complaint, he does not know who to talk to. When the men wear uniforms, it saves time."

But Bailey would not wear a uniform. Just why he shies at

brass buttons and blue cloth, no one but Bailey knows. Maybe he thinks it don't become a fat man. So Bailey failed to report for duty yesterday, and his name was dropped from the pay roll. The chief will insist on his men wearing uniforms. It is understood that he will make up his mind in a few days who is to be permanently named sergeant in Bailey's place.

Muskogee Times-Democrat, February 18, 1913.
Muskogee, Oklahoma.

GIRL COP IS TOO ATTRACTIVE; FIRED

Portsmouth, N. H., December 30-Miss Vern Virginia Bash, the policewoman of this city, has been discharged. The reason given is that she obtained no results and was too young and attractive. She was paid $800 a year by the Civic association. She came from Waynesburg, Pa.

Logansport Pharos-Reporter, December 30, 1913.
Logansport, Indiana.

What do you do when the police department is in possession of evidence that implicates you in a crime in which they are investigating? Faced with this question, the suspect in the next story decides to embark upon a brazen scheme to steal such evidence right out of a police station.

DOPES OFFICER, GETS FINGER-PRINT RECORD

OKLAHOMA CITY, Dec. 30-A stranger, who represented himself as a postoffice [sic] inspector, entered the police here today, gave an officer a narcotized cigarette, and while the latter was unconscious walked out with finger print evidence obtained by the police from a bottle of explosive used in a recent robbery of a Santa Fe mail car near Edmond, Okla.

The stranger introduced himself as "Mr. William." H. A. Murphy, Bertillion expert, produced the finger prints and was talking to the man about the robbery when the latter offered him a cigarette, the officer related after two physicians had

81

spent three hours reviving him.

Murphy said that after lighting the cigarette he talked a few minutes to the man and then lost consciousness. His last remembrance, he said, was seeing the stranger reach for the prints and hearing him say: "Well, I got you that time."

New Castle News, December 30, 1922.
New Castle, Pennsylvania.

Coming into contact with criminals on a daily basis, the duties of a guard working in a jail or prison can prove just as dangerous, if not more so, than those of a police officer working the streets.

MURDERER ATTACKS GUARD WHO BEARS MESSAGE OF LIFE

BUFFALO, Dec. 30.-When John Geise, jail guard, went to tell John Verosky of East Pittsburgh, held for murdering his 22-year -old wife, Barbara Stengel Verosky, here last June that he would go to Mattewan instead of the electric chair, the prisoner, according to jail officials, attacked the guard and attempted to strangle him.

Steps will be taken immediately to commit Verosky to the state hospital for the criminal insane.

Verosky is accused of the most horrible murder in the crime annals of Erie county. He followed his estranged wife to Buffalo and found her employed in a beauty parlor. Late one afternoon he entered the parlor, grabbed her by the neck and poured a pint of carbolic acid down her throat and burned out her eyes.

New Castle News, December 30, 1922.
New Castle, Pennsylvania.

By the standards of today, the following case appears somewhat trivial. Nonetheless, such health laws are usually enacted for good reason.

SAYS LAW AGAINST SKIMMED MILK
IS OBSOLETE

SPRINGFIELD, O., July 24.-W. H. Bitney, general manager of a local dairy company was found guilty in police court here today of selling unclean milk and also selling skimmed milk. He was fined $100 and costs in each case.

The charges were filed several weeks ago in the campaign of the local health department to secure better milk for Springfield. In the skimmed milk case the company says it was doing what has been in practice in Ohio and other states for years that is standardizing the milk. It contended that the statute prohibiting the selling of skimmed milk was obsolete.

The Daily Republican-News, July 24, 1919.
Hamilton, Ohio.

Common sense tells us that it is very difficult, if not impossible, to keep a secret while confined to a jail cell. How the following individual intended to keep her secret hidden is anybody's guess.

REFUSES TO BATHE IN JAIL;
"MAN" PRISONER A WOMAN

Wilkes-Barre, July 15.-A Luzerne county jail prisoner, "Abe Jersavage," held on a charge of disorderly conduct, refused yesterday to take a bath in the presence of the guards. When the guards attempted to use force the prisoner declared she was a woman.

The woman wore a man's attire. Her hair was cropped close to her head and everything about her appearance indicated that she was a man. She refused to tell anything about herself.

Lock Haven Express, July 15, 1916.
Lock Haven, Pennsylvania.

Prison escapes have been the plot of so many portrayals by the entertainment industry that the subject has become a major component of popular culture in America. In the following pair of accounts, two prisoners discover a way to beat the system, at least temporarily.

DUMMY SHERIFF AND DUMMY PRISONER

Potosi, Mo., Dec. 24-Chris Yarborough, who was in jail here on the charge of horse stealing, effected his escape by a clever ruse which completely deceived Sheriff Jeff Higginbotham.

Yarborough prepared a dummy to represent himself in bed asleep, and when the sheriff entered the cell to take away the supper dishes and close the prison for the night Yarborough slipped out of the bull pen, where he had concealed himself, and out of the open door leading to the street and liberty.

The disappearance of the prisoner was not discovered until some time later, when John Bean, who is also held in custody, told the sheriff that Yarborough had escaped. Higginbotham was at first incredulous, but on investigation found that he had locked a dummy in Yarborough's cell. He immediately organized a posse and went in pursuit of the fugitive.

The Decatur Review, December 23, 1903.
Decatur, Illinois.

FORGERY PRISONER MAKES
GETAWAY FROM CAMP

MONTGOMERY, Ala., Dec. 31.-C. E. Leon, alias R. W. Jones, serving from two to three years for second degree forgery, made his way to freedom from the Aldrich Alabama prison camp yesterday, according to word received today by the state convict department.

Leon was hospital steward at the camp. He secured an official order on file and erased the name of a paroled convict, substituting his own name. It readily was accepted by the authorities at the camp, and Leon walked out on a ten days parole. He is said to be wanted by the Cincinnati police.

The Indianapolis Sunday Star, January 1, 1922.
Indianapolis, Indiana.

While the breakouts in the previous articles proved successful, the inmates of a jail in Valparaiso, Indiana, had their escape plans thwarted by one tough lady.

WOMAN AVERTS JAIL-BREAKING

Valparaiso, Ind., Oct. 19.-A woman made herself the heroine of Valparaiso yesterday through preventing a wholesale jail delivery. Pointing a revolver at several men who were fleeing, she drove them back into their cells, then locked them in. Meantime her husband, Sheriff Wood, pursued two men who got outside the jail before the attempt at jail breaking was discovered. The two, Albert Tralina and James McCarthy, arrested as tramps, were recaptured by the sheriff and a posse near South Wanatah. They sawed through the bars of the jail cage. While her husband was pursuing them the sheriff's wife sat on guard at the jail with pistol in hand.

The Weekly Sentinel, October 23, 1912.
Fort Wayne, Indiana.

As attested by the following excerpt, the rules and regulations of American prisons during the early twentieth century were a great deal harsher than we are accustomed to today.

MAY STOP WOMEN FROM TALKING

Albany NY. Feb 19-Inmates of the state prison for women at Auburn will probably lose their recently granted liberty of conversation. The rule permitting general conversation at meals and in the shop was adopted at the suggestion of two young women investigators who voluntarily entered the prison several months ago to study conditions there. The chief matron's report today shows that the rule has not worked well because the opportunity has been used by some to engage in vile language and degraded discussions.

Prison Commissioner Wade today recommended that the conversational period be limited to half an hour each morning and again at the close of the day.

The Daily Review, February 19, 1914.

Decatur, Illinois.

Today, it is common for insurance companies, employers, etc., to hire private investigators to provide proof of a person committing fraud by fabricating personal injuries. In 1921, an investigation of this type led to one of the earliest examples of motion picture evidence being used in a courtroom.

FILM OF FAIR PLAINTIFF USED TO DEFEND SUIT

New York, Dec. 27-In preparation for the fight at the retrial of the suit of Miss Marie L. Frye, of Peekskill, against Walter B. Gage for $50,000 damages for injuries she alleges she suffered when run down by an automobile driven by Mr. Gage, motion pictures of Miss Frye walking down a long flight of steps were taken at the direction of detectives at Coney Island last summer, it was brought out today at the retrial.

Miss Frye was run down by Mr. Gage's automobile in Peekskill in November 1920. She alleges that she was permanently incapacitated. The retrial of her suit has been in progress before Supreme Court Justice J. Addison Young, in White Plains.

Two women detectives, who took up residence on the same block in Brooklyn as Miss Frye last summer and struck up an acquaintance with her, introduced snapshots of the young woman on parties at Coney Island, to which they said they had accompanied her. Mrs. Lillian Zeldt, one of the detectives, told today of the motion picture evidence.

In the course of one of the parties, she said, she had arranged to have a motion picture cameraman at the bottom of a long flight of steps. She held Miss Frye back, she testified, until the steps were cleared and then the two started down. The young woman was half way down the steps, Mrs. Zeldt said, before she noticed the camera. Then the detective swore she exclaimed:

"Oh my God! There is some one out to get me!" She pulled her hat over her face until she was out of range. At the foot of the step, however, Miss Frye is said to have posed for a snapshot taken by the detective.

Mrs. Zeldt testified that she had seen the motion pictures made on the occasion referred to, and that they fairly represented the incident. In view of this assertion, Justice overruled the objection made by Thomas J. O'Neill, attorney for Miss Frye, that motion pictures at easily "faked," and that the pictures should not be submitted.

The Washington Post, December 28, 1921.
Washington, D. C.

The next four accounts, including one lengthy dissertation concerning a misguided fan of a stage actress, relate the various natures of civil disputes. Although all of the following incidents took place over ninety years ago, these stories are not much unlike those appearing regularly in the newspapers of today, thus attesting to the fact that nothing ever truly changes.

The Old Story-With Variations.

John Williamson, an employe [sic] of Butler Bros.' restaurant, is charged by Miss Emma Grubbs, a well connected young lady of Lincoln, with being the father of an illegitimate child, of which she is about to become the mother. Williamson has visited Lincoln, and Miss Grubbs has visited here. Williamson, however, says that he is innocent of the charge. The young lady swore out a warrant Monday for his arrest, and Marshall Hewes received a telegram authorizing him to place the defendant under arrest. Williamson suspected that something would be done, and when he saw the officers enter the door of the restaurant, he slid out the back door, and ran out of town down towards the river. The officers followed, but lost track of him among the trees and underbrush along the river, and when it became dark gave up the search. Williamson's father is a respectable old gentleman living on Dr. Waltz's farm, just across the river, near the county bridge.

The Saturday Herald, April 21, 1883.

Decatur, Illinois.

FORSAKES HIS CHILDREN.

NEW YORK, April 14.-An interesting trial to determine a rich man's sanity is in progress before a sheriff's jury in this city. A man whose mental condition is in question is Mr. John Gill, of 149 East Twenty-Sixth street, eighty-two years of age, and said to be worth $300,000. The writ of inquiry was issued upon petition of his children.

Jane Poole, one of the daughters of Mr. Gill, testified that up to January, 1881, she was on good terms with her father, but that subsequently he became completely under the influence of two sisters, servants in his household, named Alice and Harriet Woodhull. These two had prevented him from seeing his children. Alice Woodhull, it was testified, had obtained possession of all of Mr. Gill's moneys, income and securities; she held his bonds, cut off the coupons, and ordered his children out of the house when they came to see him.

Mr. Gill, a large man with a flowing white beard, was next examined personally. He said that he hired Alice and Harriet Woodhull for $30 a month; that he had sold the house to Alice for $7,000; that Alice and her sister had been with him for ten or twelve years; that his wife died ten or eleven years ago, and that she bore him four or five children. [There are six children living, and there were fifteen in all.] When asked whether he attended church, he said, "I know nothing about the church." When asked, "Why not?" he replied: "That's my business."

When other questions were asked him he became impatient. He said he had but one bond and, asked regarding its appearance he said, "Oh, you know what it looks like." He would not tell what his property was and asked where his bank book was, he said, "I don't tell everybody where my bank-book is; I do not see why I should answer all these questions, that's my business." When Mr. Pryor asked, "Are you fond of

Alice?" he answered, "What's that to you?" In reply to Mr. Pryor's inquiry whether he knew the object of bringing him to court, and whether he knew that it was an inquest as to his sanity, he said, "If I ain't insane you folks will make me so before I get through."

The Saturday Herald, April 21, 1883.
Decatur, Illinois.

SUED BY A SWELL.

Pretty, petite Fannie Stevens, who played one of the "tailor-made young women" in "A Hole in the Ground" at the Park Theater last week, received a bulky, legal-looking package last Friday morning.

The little lady was surprised and frightened to find that she had been sued for $10,000. Not until she had read the papers did she grasp the situation. Then she found that she had been sued for breach of promise by Edmond J. Levy, damages being laid at the above figure.

Charles H. Hoyt, author and manager of the play, was seen at the close of last night's performance by a GLOBE reporter, and in answer to the question as to the truth of the statement that Miss Stevens is to figure as the defendant in a breach of promise suit, said that so far as he knew the story is true.

"The history of the young man's meeting and subsequent infatuation of the fair tailor-made girl," said Mr. Hoyt, "is, so far as can be ascertained, as follows; While the play was running in New York Mr. Levy went to see it, liked the plot and cast, and fell desperately in love with Miss Stevens. He was so smitten that he was determined to meet and become acquainted with her. He had the good sense and pride to accomplish this desired end in a legitimate and perfectly fair manner. He looked around and found some one who was acquainted with Miss Stevens and with himself. This was not a difficult matter, for as you know Miss Stevens is a well acquainted lady and one whose reputation is above reproach. She is indeed a member of the best society, besides being a remarkably clever actress. I have known her a long time and am perhaps better acquainted with her than any other lady in my company.

Levy was successful in obtaining an introduction, and forthwith began to pay close attention to her. Miss Stevens did not find his attentions disagreeable, for he was not ostentatious in his demeanor; on the other hand he always acted the part of a perfect gentleman, and so far as I know never did or said anything unbecoming a gentleman.

"He was very badly smitten, of course, and attended the theatre regularly, and sent flowers to her by way of the stage entrance. Now you know as well as any one that when flowers are sent in at the stage door of a theatre they are not going to be sent back. He met her frequently, talked with her, I suppose, and about four weeks ago asked her to become Mrs. Levy.

"To the best of my belief that was the first intimation she had of his intentions. She had supposed that he was simply an admirer, as were many other young gentlemen. She replied to his proposal that though she had found his society very pleasant, she had no desire to forsake the stage. She was not aware that she had ever given him any reason to suppose she would marry him. She liked him, but could not accept his proposal.

"Mr. Levy took his refusal in a quiet manner, made no demonstration of anger or broken-heartedness, and continued to send her flowers and fruit. I do not think he endeavored to see her after that, however, nor do I think he persisted in his proposal, in fact he acted just as he always had, as a perfectly well-bred gentleman.

"Last Sunday after my company had gone down to the Grand Central depot to take the train for our trip over to Boston, Levy appeared and asked me if I had any objection to his coming over to Boston on the same train. I told him that the county is a free one, and the trains run, so I guessed he might come to Boston if he chose. So he came over. He was acquainted with a number of the members of the company, who had found him a pleasant man, and so his trip was a pleasant one to all. He secured quarters at the Adams House, and as you know, has brought suit for breach of promise.

"I have this to say about that part of it. I think he has become intimate with a number of Boston sells, and through their influence has committed an action he will regret when he comes to think more carefully of it. He belongs to a prominent family in New York, and lives, I think, in Thirty-sixth street."

Miss Steven was in her room donning her street costume, and when word was sent her that a GLOBE reporter wished to see her she responded that she would appear at once.

She was asked about the matter, and at first refused to say anything, but at last said that the story was one which had embarrassed her not a little and caused her no end of annoyance. She was asked about Mr. Levy's proposal, and amid blushes and nervous movements of her hands said she could not make a statement.

She did say, however, that she believed Mr. Levy a perfect gentleman. He had never in the slightest sense overstepped the limits of propriety. She was unconscious of his deep infatuation for her until the propo[s]al came. She does not think that he commenced the breach of promise proceedings wholly uninfluenced to do so, for if he has it is the first ungentlemanly act she ever knew of him.

The possible scandal which might arise from the story she could not afford to encounter, and the least said about the matter the better. At any rate, her acceptance or refusal of Mr. Levy's proposal was a private matter. She did not know who she would employ as counsel.

The Boston Sunday Globe, November 6, 1887,
Boston, Massachusetts.

CLAIMS $5,000 FOR MAID'S DELAY

Winnipeg, Man. July 3-The Grand Trunk Pacific Railway has received a demand from a Saskatchewan farmer for $5,000 because of an alleged delay of six weeks in securing transportation for his housekeeper, who was coming from Louisiana. A later letter compromised on $1,000.

"Please do not make me go to the law about this," the farmer urged, "for I know that you have more money than I have. Just send the money along and I will call it square."

The Bismarck Tribune, July 3, 1920.
Bismarck, North Dakota.

Finally, we come to the last story of this chapter. It is a tale in which the legitimacy of a will is entangled within a web of suspicious circumstances.

AN ENTERPRISING CORPSE.
A Missouri Dead Man Signs His Own Will.

An interesting will case, which has been pending in the courts in Franklin county for years past, rivals in its nature anything of the sort, possibly ever heard of in the history of the present age. The circumstances, as gathered from one of the attorneys engaged for the defense (outside of the court room), are briefly as follows: Some time ago there lived in the town of Washington an old bachelor, who possessed a considerable amount of property, and had no relatives save one who it is said, was needy. The individual (bachelor) was taken quite ill, and was advised to make his will, which he did, bequeathing all of his estate to the children of a friend. The news became generally known in the town of the manner in which the testator had disposed of his property, leaving out any consideration to his kindred friend. While the man still lingered on his bed of sickness, it was made up among some of the friends of the relative that three of them should visit the sick man and advise him to make a second will, with provisions for the relief of the kinsman. Consent being given, the parties, who it is said, were all on a "tight," and who had no personal interest in the matter save the good feeling they entertained for the neglected friend, appointed one of their number to write. The table was drawn up close to the bedside of the sick man, who as well as he could, dictated the nature of his bequest. Before the conclusion and signing of the will the man died. One of the party remarked to the scribe "that it was useless to go on, as the man was dead as h--l." However, after its conclusion, the dead man was lifted up in a sitting posture and held, the pen was placed between his fingers, and made to trace his name, after which the question was asked, "Do you acknowledge this to be your signature and last will," etc.? The dead man, by the aid of those who held him up, nodded assent. The corpse was then quietly laid down, and the individuals signed their respective names as witnesses to the instrument. The trio who witnessed the will are now all dead, and the only seeming trouble is the proper construction of the will, which, under the circumstances and under the influence of an intoxicated brain, the scribe somewhat blended in meaning.

Semi-Weekly Wisconsin, January 1, 1870.
Milwaukee, Wisconsin.

Chapter Six
Strange Accidents & Narrow Escapes

In addition to accounts concerning crime and punishment, accidents and brushes with misfortune are common themes for newspaper articles. In this chapter, a number of such incidents are related in the manner in which they were originally published.

Unless you have been living in a cave for the past twenty years, it is a fair assumption that you have been exposed to countless hours of television footage involving police chases and examples of reckless driving caught on camera. During this timeframe, the reporting of such incidents by the media has become commonplace. In the following excerpt, however, we find that such foolhardy conduct has been committed since at least the horse and buggy era.

Caused by Reckless Driving.

READING, Pa., May 12.-Five young men of this city hired a double team of Liveryman J. S. Moyer, under pretense of going to Birdsboro, but instead they drove recklessly in the suburbs. In going down Chestnut street the team became uncontrollable and dashed into a telegraph post. One of the horses was killed and the other badly crippled. Joseph Kinney, who was driving, was thrown upon his head and severely injured. The carriage was demolished.

Lebanon Daily News, May 12, 1891.
Lebanon, Pennsylvania.

With its spinning blade capable of slicing effortlessly through the hardest of woods, the inherit dangers of a circular saw leaves little to the imagination.

Badly Cut Up.

LITTLE FALLS, Minn., June 24.-Guy Johnson a saw mill man, employed at Long's mill, at Curtis, was cut in two by the circular saw, death, of course, being instantaneous. He was unmarried, and has relatives living near Duluth.

The Eau Claire Sunday-Weekly Leader, June 26, 1892.
Eau Claire, Wisconsin.

While the previous tale had a tragic ending, the next example relates a farmer's miraculous escape from death during a similar accident.

FARMER MISSED DEATH BY A HAIR'S BREADTH.

Reading, Dec. 24.-While Beltmer Weitzel, a farmer living up in Tuipehocken Creek, was working in his sawmill, a circular saw flew off with terrific force, passing directly over his head and cutting off several locks of his hair.

The saw passed through a rail fence 150 feet away and was only stopped in its flight by a large boulder thirty feet beyond the fence.

The Post-Standard, December 25, 1899.
Syracuse, New York.

The following account describes an accident caused when a pair of horses panicked while pulling a street sweeper.

Street Sweeper vs. Beer Wagon.

William Macauley is the driver of one those ingenious contrivances that sweep the refuse from the public thoroughfares. As Mr. Macauley was head up Shawmut avenue yesterday his pair of steeds took fright and set up a terrible gallop. In another minute they had gone plump into a beer wagon, driven by a phlegmatic Teuton, and Mr. Macauley was thrown into the gutter. He was picked up pretty badly done up. Dr. Cushing was called. His injuries necessitating careful nursing. Mr. Macualey was removed to the City Hospital.

The Boston Sunday Globe, November 6, 1887.
Boston, Massachusetts.

As automobiles began to share the road with horses, it was inevitable that certain instances of chaos would erupt between these two modes of transportation.

Exciting Runaway.

Considerable excitement was caused on Spring street Sunday evening when a horse driven by Barney Lahrman and Allie Bennett, of Medora, ran away. It became frightened near G.S. Gray's residence at an automobile and began kicking and plunging at a fearful rate which caused Lahrman to crawl over the back of the seat and jump out at the rear of the buggy. Bennett tried his best to quiet the horse but could not do so. It ran up the steep embankment at Willis Robbins' residence and then made a quick turn toward Jas. Kent's residence where the buggy collided with a tree with such force that the horse was freed from the buggy and continued its run along different streets, until it was stopped at Buening's livery stable. Bennett, who so pluckily remained with the rig, jumped out just before the buggy struck the tree and was uninjured. The buggy was turned over and was pretty badly wrenched, but aside from breaking the shafts and swingletree no other damage was done.

Brownstown Banner, May 21, 1913.
Brownstown, Indiana.

HUNTINGTON, Ind. Jan. 23-Lewis Everding, an employe of the Orton-Steinbrenner plant, who lives south of the city, narrowly escaped serious injury or death Tuesday evening when his buggy was broken in two in a collision with an automobile. The automobile, driven by John Snyder, an employe of George Kapp, a milkman, struck the buggy from behind. The buggy buckled and Everding was caught in it. Then the horse, which had been knocked to its knees, ran away, carrying Everding in the smashed buggy. He finally succeeded in getting clear, but in doing so was thrown violently, rolling into the ditch at the side of the road. Snyder is making arrangements to pay for the damage.

The Fort Wayne News And Sentinel, January 23, 1919.
Fort Wayne, Indiana.

The dawn of automobile ownership for the masses brought with it many new dangers to everyday life. As related in the following accounts, many of these hazards lurked in the shadows awaiting the opportunity to pounce upon the uninitiated.

Ran Over by His Own Auto.

Dr. Kendell, of Crothersville, met with a peculiar accident Monday. He stepped in front of his machine to crank it and one of the speed levers had been left in position. As soon as the engine started, the machine plunged forward, knocking the doctor down and ran over him, but he escaped serious injury. The auto ran against an embankment and stopped.

Brownstown Banner, May 21, 1913.
Brownstown, Indiana.

AUTO RUNS AWAY FROM FARMER

Hetland, S. D. July 3.-While preparing to return home after attending a show here a cattle buyer had an experience with a runaway automobile. He cranked up the car and left the engine running while he went after his coat. He returned to find his auto "beating it" toward the owner's home at Arlington, and fracturing all the traffic laws of the town and state. The wild car crashed through two fences and then jumped into a lake. Two-thirds of the men in town, all the small boys and a team of horses were mobilized to tow the car to dry land.

The Bismarck Tribune, July 3, 1920.
Bismarck, North Dakota.

When it comes to consumer goods, we live in an incredibly safer world today than what was considered normal just one-hundred years ago. One such example is the enforcement of flammability standards for most clothing currently sold on the market, an unappreciated blessing that would have most likely prevented the following tragedy involving a popular fashion item of the day.

DEATH DUE TO BALLOON SLEEVES.

The balloon sleeve has caused the burning to death of two women in Philadelphia, mother and daughter. Miss Helena Riggs, 19, was shockingly burned at her home and died the next day. Mrs. Emma Riggs, 47, was the second victim and her clothing was ignited in her attempt to save her daughter. It was the sleeves of the latter that caught fire at a gas stove and caused the fatal burning of both. They were prominent in West Philadelphia social circles.

The Weekly Wisconsin, September 21, 1895.
Milwaukee, Wisconsin.

The following pair of stories relates the exploits of two extremely lucky individuals.

NARROW ESCAPE

Tom Martin, a young Irishman employed on the Southern Indiana grout train, which hauls crushed stone from the crusher at Rockledge and distributes it along the line, had a close call for his life Tuesday a.m. The train was running eastward at good speed, when about three miles west of Bedford the hook end of a long steel cable used to drag the big plow which pushes the grout off the train dropped overboard between the two cars. The hook soon caught on a cross tie, and the cable went wiggling and squirming along the tops of the cars at a lively rate. A shout of warning went up, and all the workmen succeeded in getting out of the way except Martin.

He started to run, but was caught in the toils and tumbled off in the ditch, receiving bruises about the head and a severe gash across the cap of the left knee. The train was soon stopped, and Martin picked up and brought to this city, where he was left in charge of a fellow workman until his injuries could be dressed by the company surgeon.

The Bedford Weekly Mail, April 14, 1899.
Bedford, Indiana.

MUST HAVE NINE LIVES.

Eldora, Ia., Aug. 30.-The proverbial cat has nine lives, but Henry Shafer, of this city, is a human exponent of this persistent existence.

Twice struck by lightning, terribly injured by the premature explosion of a cannon, losing an eye, one arm and three fingers thereby, having fallen headlong off the top of a high cliff, having figured in a mine cavein [*sic*] and several runaways, the man still survives. Blind in one eye, short of an arm and with but two fingers on the remaining hand, he supports a big family and is contented and happy.

The saying that lightning never strikes twice in the same place came very nearly being disproved last night when Shafer for the second time was the mark for a bolt. But, metaphorically, it never feazed him-just stunned him a bit. He was around again a few minutes after the shock, thus apparently proving the belief that he bears a charmed life. The other time when Shafer was struck he lay stunned on the sidewalk all night in a drenching rain.

The O'Brien County Bell, August 31, 1905.
Primghar, Iowa.

(Note-feaze, or feeze, is defined as a state of panic.)

Chapter Seven
Odds and Ends

Prior to the internet, newspapers had the most diverse audience of any published work. With the general public as its readers, it was necessary for these publications to appeal to people of all walks of life and backgrounds. As such, many stories included in most editions were far removed from the main headlines.

In the following account, we learn of a man that somehow managed to get himself lost in a city's sewer system.

LOST IN A SEWER

Steubenville, O[H]., Dec. 25.-After wandering 36 hours in big sewer mains under the streets of the city, unable to make his cries for help heard, Steve Hobolo, 23, an employe [sic] at the Carnegie steel plant, was rescued, insane. It is believed Hobolo in some way crawled into a sewer entrance at the river bank and was unable to find his way out. Passersby finally heard faint noises under a manhole and pulled Hobolo out, nearly starved and raving.

Van Wert Daily Bulletin, December 26, 1913.
Van Wert, Ohio.

A timeless adage tells us that there are only two things certain in life; death and taxes. During the early part of the twentieth century, a fervent suffrage movement existed in the United States, the aim of which was to give women the right to vote. The following article relates the platform of the Suffrage Congressional Union and Woman Suffrage Association to convince women to withhold paying their income taxes in protest of government policy. Although the passage of the Nineteenth Amendment in 1920 gave women the right to vote in the United States, they never became exempt from paying income taxes.

TO RESIST INCOME TAX

Washington, Dec. 31-"Resistance" on the part of the women of the country to the federal income tax law, despite the government's announced intention to impose fines of $1,000 for each failure to report incomes, will receive the encouragement of the Suffragist Congressional union, it is announced in a statement issued by the organization headquarters here. Resistance to the law, it is declared, would be thoroughly justified from a moral standpoint.

The statement coming as it does upon the heels of the suggestion of Rev. Anna Howard Shaw, president of the National Woman Suffrage association, that the unenfranchised women of the country decline to aid the government in collecting taxes upon their incomes, caused a sensation in congressional, treasury, and suffragist circles.

Imposition of an income tax on women, the women's statement asserts, has made them realize afresh their helplessness under the government. To tax the women without granting them representation, it is said, would be an act of "intolerable injustice."

"Resistance to the income tax law," the statement adds, "would have excellent educational value, and would be thoroughly justified morally."

It is stated in conclusion, however, that the union will not undertake to organize a protest against the law.

Treasury officials are preparing to ferret out taxable possessions even if the women withhold statements. There is a provision which appropriates $800,000 for collecting the tax and states that the commissioner of internal revenue my pay such sums as he deems necessary for "information, detection and bringing to trial and punishment, persons guilty of violating the provisions of this section or conniving at the same."

National Democrat, January 1, 1914.
Des Moines, Iowa.

101

Concurrent with the work of suffragists in the United States, a similar movement took place in the United Kingdom. While the activities of the women's suffrage movement in America remained relatively peaceful in nature, the militaristic undertones prevalent within the campaign across the Atlantic are related in the next account. In 1928, women, twenty-one years of age and older, living in the United Kingdom received the same voting rights as men.

Thirty Million Damage Done by Suffragettes

London, November 12-Thirty million dollars damages has been caused by the warfare of the militant suffragettes since they began their campaign of violence in England, Scotland, and Wales, according to figures compiled here today. The greater part of this was caused by fires set by the "arson squad," and explosions caused by bombs, but severe loss has been caused to business in many places.

Logansport Pharos-Reporter, November 12, 1913.

Logansport, Indiana.

Silent films became an incredibly popular form of amusement during the early twentieth century. As with most forms of entertainment, however, it did not escape an occasional brush with controversy.

"SEE" BAD WORDS ON FILMS.
Lip-Readers Object to Expressions Used By Players in Moving Pictures.

Cleveland. Dec 12-Deaf mutes are complaining against the use of profane and indecent expressions by players in moving picture films and will ask for a rigid censorship by the manufacturers.

Mrs. Elmer E. Bates, for many years a teacher of deaf and dumb and an expert in the art of lip reading declares that these shows are the chief source of amusement for the deaf, and they are prevented from enjoying them because they are able to understand what is being said by the characters on the screens. Mrs. Bates made a tour of the downtown shows yesterday, accompanied by a reporter who wrote down the picture talk and at times the language was such that she had to stop.

Mayor Baehr admits that the question is too deep for him.

The Washington Post, December 13, 1910.
Washington, D. C.

The next two tales relate a pair of bizarre, but apparently factual, medical cases.

HAT PIN TAKEN FROM BOY'S BODY

Grundy Center, April 19.-(Special)-Surgeons have just removed a lady's hat pin, six inches in length, form the abdomen of John Welchers, an 18-year-old boy who lives in Pleasant Valley township. For some years Welchers has been afflicted at times with excruciating pains. A recent attack was so severe that when physicians failed to relieve the pain by medication they decided upon an operation. The knob, or beaded point, of the pin was nearest the surface of the body and the shaft was imbedded in the flesh, while the point was near the intestines, which fortunately it had not penetrated. Rust and mineral matter had accumulated upon the pin until it was about the size of a lead pencil. How this foreign object came to be in the body is a problem which both the young man and his parents are unable to solve. The supposition is that it gained admission in some way while the boy was a baby. For several years the sharp pains in the region of the abdomen led to the belief that the patient was suffering from appendicitis, but this was the only symptom that would justify such a diagnosis. The young man is troubled with another growth on his right side and it may be necessary to have an operation to determine what the trouble is in that part of the body. Another hat pin may be found.

Semi Weekly Waterloo Courier, April 23, 1907.
Waterloo, Iowa.

CRICKET IN ONE OF HIS EARS.

FLEMINGTON, N. J., Dec. 31.-Charles Blazier of High Bridge, who has been practically deaf for six months and recently so deaf he could not hear a gun fired, has recovered his hearing.

Blazier lay down on the grass under a tree last Summer, and went to sleep. He felt a buzzing in his ear when he arose, and within a short time was almost insane. He said there were noises in his head as if a boiler factory, several county bands, and many horse fiddles were trying to outdo each other. He claimed the noises were in his brain. For almost two weeks this kept up. Blazier could not sleep, nor could he remain quiet during this time.

The noises stopped at last, but he found he could not hear out of his right ear, and later the left one also failed him. He at first could hear indistinctly, but later this also failed. The doctors could not fathom the case. The fact that Blazier had insisted that the noises were in his head threw them off.

Dr. M. D. Knight a few days ago determined to investigate the ears. After some trouble the doctor located a foreign substance and removed it. It proved to be the remains of a cricket. Within a short time after the cricket was taken out Blazier began to improve, and now, after the lapse of a couple of days, he can hear almost as well as ever.

The New York Times, January 1, 1900.
New York City, New York.

From the following article, one can assume that the growth of the mail order business was taking its toll on local proprietors, thus necessitating an extraordinary response.

Mail Order Catalogs as One Big Bonfire.

CEDAR FALLS, Ia., Jan. 29.-Professor F. L. McCreary, secretary of the Commercial Club, has inaugurated a new idea of advertising the city and also one which he thinks will benefit the local merchant. As soon as the weather will permit, a large gathering will be held in front of the Commercial club rooms to which everybody will be invited. A immense bonfire will be built and each and every person in the city will be asked to bring all the mail order catalogs they can find and consign them to the flames, making one of the grandest, as well as one the most useful conflagrations ever witnessed here. The Cedars Falls band will head a procession to the spot in which the catalogs will be hauled on a funeral car. The band will play a funeral dirge while the catalogs are being consumed.

Atlantic News-Telegraph, January 30, 1912.
Atlantic, Iowa.

An unorthodox effort by health officials to prevent the spread of fever during 1897 is described by the next narrative.

Looks Like Targets.
Several letters from New Orleans were received in Waterloo this morning. The envelopes and letters look as though they had been used as targets by the Waterloo gun club. The perforations were made by the authorities, however, to kill the danger of fever germs lurking in the atmosphere of the southern city.

The Waterloo Courier, October 13, 1897.
Waterloo, Iowa.

Over the past twenty years, a general decline in the number of yearly school days has occurred within the public school system. The writer of the following article recognizes some of the consequences of a limited school year, using the interesting approach of comparing a school system with a private enterprise.

LONGER SCHOOL DAYS ARE URGED
Chicago, March 14.-Longer school days with sessions throughout the summer months are urged in an article in the current number of the School Review issued at the University of Chicago.

Moral and scholastic delinquency would be prevented and

economic waste in school management would be eliminated under such a plan according to the article.

"City children are becoming more and more helpless as the result of the idleness imposed upon them by city life," says the article. "The boys, at least, are exposed through their long evenings and holidays to the vicious influence of the street.

"If a private corporation valued at $2,000,000,000 occupied in production but 1,000 hours, 6 hours a day for approximately 166 days, the manager of that corporation would estimate his annual loss to be in the neighborhood of $30,000,000."

The article urges the employment of vocational teachers the year around.

The Morning Echo, March 15, 1914.
Bakersfield, California.

While the culprit of the next tale may not have eaten "a meal fit for a king," he was nonetheless able to feast upon one worthy of a president.

Mystery of the Missing Reindeer Is Unsolved

"WHO ate the reindeer?" is the question that is agitating the department of the interior. It is a deep, dark mystery. Herbert Meyer, private secretary to the secretary of interior, affects to believe that the matter is one of no moment. But when he is pressed into discussion of the subject his face wears the expression seen upon the face of the cat after its justly celebrated interview with the canary. But he is the one member of the secretary's immediate official family who has produced an alibi for himself. Private secretaries, in the very nature of their work, are experts in alibis.

The story of the missing reindeer starts with the beginning of the winter's social activities in Washington. For the first time in several years official Washington determined to resume the old practice of having cabinet dinners. That is, each cabinet officer in turn was to give a dinner to the president and Mrs. Wilson.

Bright young men about the department concluded that here was a chance to pull a clever stunt and incidentally advertise the resources of Alaska. Stephen T. Mather, a young millionaire who puts in some 14 hours a day at work as assistant to the secretary, put the idea into effect. He got William T. Loop, who is in charge of the Alaska school and reindeer service, to import a shipment of reindeer meat from Alaska via Seattle, and it was put in cold storage awaiting Secretary Lane's cabinet dinner.

The secretary was called West unexpectedly, and it was necessary to postpone the feast. Therefore the cold-storage warehouse had the custody of the precious meat for some time.

When the dinner date approached someone thought to check up on the meat. A delegation visited the butcher shop where it had been stored. Mother Hubbard's sensations on discovering the bareness of her cupboard had nothing on the sensations of the delegation. The meat, so the butcher said, had been withdrawn by order of the secretary. The secretary, when this was reported to him, was mystified, but since several have authority to do things in his name he concluded to remain mystified. Inquiries might prove embarrassing.

So it was that President Wilson had something else to eat when he tucked his legs under Secretary Lane's table. Alaska reindeer did not appear on the menu.

Attica Daily Tribune, June 24, 1916.
Attica, Indiana.

Frustration concerning the degradation of the English language during the early twentieth century resulted in the following proposal, which called for the creation of an unparalleled anti-cruelty association.

Would Form Society To Prevent Cruelty To English Language

Chicago, November 28.-Joseph Jastrow, of the University of Wisconsin, speaking here today before the National Council of Theaters of English, referred to the possibility of a society for the prevention of cruelty to the English language.

Professor Jastrow told the result of an inquiry as to what would be the outcome if fifty objectionable expressions caught in ordinary conversations were fined such amounts varying from 1 cent to $1 as seemed a fit punishment for each separate offense according to the pain inflicted on the hearer. The judges, sixty-eight in number, included twelve women. Half of the sixty-eight reside east of the Alleghenies. Among the judges were college professors, leading editors and readers for prominent publishing houses.

An average fine of nearly 43 cents for each offense was the outcome.

F. N. Scott, of the University of Michigan, whose topic was "the undefined gate," asked "of what use is it to drill pupils in grammar, to sweat over compositions, to spend month after month in the reading and study of English masterpieces, if steadily day by day some powerful disintegrating agency nullifies all that we have accomplished?"

Not even the Bible, Professor Scott said, could now compete with the daily newspaper as the most powerful and pervasive influence of our day and nation. Accordingly, Professor Scott urged that the language as well as the spirit of the newspaper should be the equal of that required of any other daily visitor to the family.

He said slang, indiscriminate use of words, violations of grammar and style, the split infinitive, the dangling participle and the abuse of "tarnspire," [sic] "inaugurate" and "enthuse" could be corrected.

The Atlanta Constitution, November 29, 1913.
Atlanta, Georgia.

Anyone who has raised a child will recall the phase all toddlers go through in which anything they grasp will go almost instantly into their mouths. While most children quickly outgrow this stage, some, as the following story attests, do not.

COULD EAT ANYTHING.

It is said that Florence Larsins, a seven-year old girl of Elwood, has the happy propensity of swallowing everything which comes her way. It is said that she recently swallowed a metal whistle and when the stomach pump was applied to remove the obstacle that several buttons, a ball of twine and numerous other articles were discovered.

The Logansport Pharos, November 9, 1906.
Logansport, Indiana.

In Chapter One, there was the story of a woman that forced her husband to sleep in the barn because he refused to bathe regularly. The individual described in the next account, however, claims to have never taken a bath.

NEVER TAKES A BATH

Frederic Cerboni, a chemist of Gelsomino, near Florence, is the most cheerful and remarkable philosopher in Italy. He had never had a bath and never washes. Soap and water, he thinks, are so much poison and washing destroys health and shortens life. He is an old man and yet in splendid health. Le Nazonine, of Florence, sent a reporter to interview him. The old man wrote out the following statement and signed it for publication:

"I am 75 years old and in the best of health and spirits. Yet I never wash, not even my face in the morning. Five years ago a towel was placed in my room, but it has not yet been changed, and there is no need of changing it. I have never taken a bath, and yet I have never been ill.

"I hold that baths, washing basins, looking glasses, brushes, soaps, sponges and all those sort of things are so much useless lumber. I have never lost a day's appetite, not a night's sleep for being without them. Can anybody say the same who has wasted their time and money at watering places and hydropathic establishments? I go to bed in my boots and wear the same clothes all year around.

"Being a chemist by profession, I know something about hygiene. Hygiene is a myth, a superstition. Microbes are killed by other microbes. That's the long and short of it. Yours truly, Frederic Cerboni."

The Logansport Pharos, November 9, 1906.
Logansport, Indiana.

Political campaigns can take a heavy toll on a candidate's health. According to the next account, the campaign season of 1906 appears to have been especially taxing.

KILLED FIVE CANDIDATES

The campaign recently closed, said by experts to have been the most nerve straining political contest in the history of America, has cost the lives of five candidates, who have succumbed from actual consumption of the life force. Rockwood Hoar candidate for congress in the Third Massachusetts, died November 1; Gen. John H. Ketcham, candidate for congress in the Twenty-first district, died Sunday; Thomas S. Delaney, candidate for assemblyman in Brooklyn, died November 2; the funeral of Wm. Hughes, judicial candidate in Brooklyn, was held yesterday and William P. Minahan, Independent candidate for congress in the Eight Wisconsin district, died eight days before the election.

The Logansport Pharos, November 9, 1906.

Logansport, Indiana.

Today, we are accustomed to the fact that the failure to pay an electric bill will lead to the service being turned off. Apparently, in 1906 this was a relatively new concept.

SHUT OFF LIGHT

The electric light department are [sic] sending notices to all consumers that in all cases were electric light bills are not payed [sic] at the specific time the lights will be immediately turned off. It is stated the amount of delinquency amounts to $7,200. Nov. 1 a new plan of determining the exact amount burned was put in operation and the charges will be kept strictly against each consumer, and rigidly collected. The purpose of sending out the notices to consumers is not, it is said to scare the consumers, but simply to notify each one of the exact condition and to fairly warn delinquents they come under the requirements ordered by the electric light department.

The Logansport Pharos, November 9, 1906.
Logansport, Indiana.

The fact that you can never have enough money is a well known proverb. The next article provides some insight into such motivations.

Why Rich Men Want More.

The reason a rich man is never satisfied with the size of his fortune is not necessarily because he has acquired a kind of hog instinct, but rather because his knowledge of affairs and his breadth of vision have grown until he sees bigger and bigger things that he wishes to do; and his ambition to accomplish is always a few leads ahead of his capital. The richest men in the world are usually the heaviest borrowers, because they are in a position to see the most to be done. Hence any man setting out to get rich might as well recognize at the beginning, that from the very nature of things, he can never hope to feel that he has enough.-Fred Kelly in The Nation's Business.

Newport Mercury, July 16, 1921.
Newport, Rhode Island.

The following account describes the final resolution of a territorial dispute between two communities.

Town Picks Up and Moves.

Topeka, Kan.-The town of Cold Springs, in Kiowa county, Oklahoma, was moved four miles in compliance with an order of the state corporation commission. The frame buildings were transported on flat cars. Two rival town sites have fought over the location of the town for several years.

The Bedford Daily Mail, January 16, 1913.
Bedford, Indiana.

It is a prisoner of war's duty to attempt an escape if the opportunity presents itself. During World War I, a large number of German prisoners were held in various internment camps around Britain. It was at one of these installations that the following escape attempt took place.

GERMAN PRISONER TRIED TO ESCAPE AS GARBAGE

LONDON, June 15 (Correspondence)-An attempt by a German prisoner to escape by concealing himself in a can of garbage was discovered at the camp at Leigh this week.

A farmer who buys all the food refuse of the camp was carting away a number of cans. The unusual weight of one of them roused his suspicions. He removed a quantity of cabbage leaves and found a German soldier beneath.

A German named Schmidt was shot and killed at Leigh a week ago while trying to escape.

Boston Evening Globe, July 1, 1915.
Boston, Massachusetts.

Discharged from the army, the subject of the next article attempts an unorthodox method to return home.

DISCOVERS MAN IN THE BOX.

San Francisco, Cal., Jan. 30.-Harry M. Prouse, a discharged soldier, formery of Oswego, N. Y., attempted to smuggle himself through to the east in a goods box. He had laid in a stock of provision, arranged with an expressman to ship the box and under cover of darkness concealed himself in the case and awaited developments.

True to his promise, the express man called for the box yesterday, but while loading the case upon his wagon he happened to catch sight of a human form. Supposing that there was a corpse in the box he drove to headquarters and notified the police.

The police officials broke open the box and soon convinced

Prouse of his folly in thus risking his life. He was discharged
with a lecture.

Davenport Weekly Leader, January 31, 1902.
Davenport, Iowa.

One of the most popular songs in America during the 1890s
was The Bowery, by Charles H. Hoyt. Relating the negative
experiences one can expect in the area of New York City known
by that name, this tune did much to further decay a declining
section of the city that had once been home to a thriving theater
district.

A SONG RUINS TRADE

NEW YORK, April 11.-The business men of the Bowery have
decided that something must be done to revive business on that
historic thoroughfare. Several conferences have been held, and
a monster meeting-the place and date of which have not been
fixed-has been decided upon, with the view of getting up a
petition to the board of aldermen to have the street's name
changed. The consensus of opinion among Bowery saloon
keepers is that if the name is changed the Bowery will soon be
its old self again.

The decadence of the Bowery is attributed to Charles H.
Hoyt's popular song of that name. The song not only charges
in a general way that "they do such things and say such things
on the Bowery," but goes into particulars and mentions barber
shops, auction stores, and other Bowery enterprises as good
things to keep away from. The Bowery merchants claim that
aspersions of the song have kept thousand of visitors to the city
from going to the Bowery.

Lebanon Semi-Weekly News, April 11, 1895.
Lebanon, Pennsylvania.

Commanding the American Expeditionary Forces during
World War I, General John J. Pershing became the most

celebrated American commander of the conflict. The popularity of his name, however, did not provide much assistance to his candy making cousins.

NAME DIDN'T HELP BUSINESS

Washington, July 3.-[F]inding that manufacturing candy did not pay, even when the product bore the name of the A. E. F. leader, Eli and Everett M. Pershing, cousins of John J. Pershing, today asked the district supreme court to adjudge their concern a[s] bankrupt. The cousins who branded their products "Pershing Candies," said they owed about $10,000 to creditor [s], which was unsecured. They gave as personal assets several army officers outfits.

The Bismarck Tribune, July 3, 1920.
Bismarck, North Dakota.

Instigated by the discovery of an amputated leg, the following story reveals the practices of discarding medical waste during the early twentieth century.

LEG MYSTERY IS NO MYSTERY

The mystery of the human leg found yesterday in a trash barrel in the rear of the Hicks' building has been solved.

It is the mummified limb of an ex-policeman. It was amputated about six months ago and came from the office of Dr. Russell Caffery, in the Hocks' [sic] building.

The fact that the leg found its way to the trash barrel is all a mistake according to Dr. Caffery. He says he was under the impression that the unoffending limb, which has created so much excitement, had been cremated, as is the custom.

After Dr. Cafferty amputated the limb about six months ago in order to save the life of a policeman who had contracted blood poison as a result of breaking his leg by slipping and falling on the sidewalk, he embalmed it and preserved it among his anatomical relics.

The limb, having served it usefulness, Dr. Caffery instructed the janitor to dispose of it, and in that way it found its way to the garbage barrel.

In an interview with Dr. Cafferty this morning he told how amputated limbs are generally disposed of, which will be a surprise to the general public.

"It is customary to place amputated limbs in the garbage barrel and they are conveyed to the garbage heap and cremated," said Dr. Cafferty. "Hundreds had gone out of this building within the last few years I am sure. We do not generally place them in the trash barrel, however, but turn them over to the garbage man, who disposes of them. It was a mere accident that this one was so placed and under ordinary circumstances nothing would have been said about it. I have violated no city ordinance."

San Antonio Gazette, April 17, 1906.
San Antonio, Texas.

Although amassing a considerable personal fortune, the subject of the next account chose to live his life in squalor.

A GERMAN MISER.

A typical miser died two weeks ago in Baden, near Vienna. His name was William Woborex. He appeared in Baden nine years ago and rented the cheapest house in town. It had but one story and only three rooms. The first evening after his arrival he went to the city park and picked up the acquaintance of Theresia Lasch, a 70-year-old widow, engaged her to keep house with him and was never known to speak to any one in the streets of Baden afterward.

For nine years he allowed none save her to enter the house. She bought him the barest necessities of life daily, and left them on his threshold. He ate food that a beggar would reject, slept on loose straw, and paid his one acquaintance just one cent a day for her services. He never had his house cleaned or windows washed, never changed the straw of his bed, and never had a new garment while in Baden.

A few days before the beginning of this last illness a fire burned down a barn very near his shanty. The neighbors hurried to his house to help him save what he might value among his apparently valueless possessions. He barred the door, however, and, brandishing an old cavalry sword behind the window, shouted that he would burn his house before he would allow any one to rob him.

When he fell ill he allowed the old woman who had brought him his food for nine years to enter to care for him on the condition that she would not charge him extra. He had no doctor, no medicine. He ordered that his funeral be made to cost as little as $5, hungered and prayed, and died with the lie on his lips that the $35 he had just given the old woman was all that he had in the world. In his big chest, hidden under the floor beneath the straw on which he died, were found $18,000 worth of coupons, 1000 shares of Belgian railway stock at $100 a share, and some $40,000 in gold, silver and notes. A last will and testament, which the old man had apparently forgotten, was also found in the chest. It bequeathed to his mother in Zierke, Germany, $5000 and the rest to the village.

The Galveston Daily News, January 2, 1891.

Galveston, Texas.

In August of 2003, a massive electrical blackout affected large portions of the northeastern United States and Ontario, Canada. In a classic example of price gouging, a large number of merchants raised the prices of gas, water, and ice exponentially, in an effort to take advantage of the situation. The next story takes place during the 1800s and relates the desperate situation that the citizens of Nantucket, Massachusetts, faced during a harsh winter. When a ship finally arrived with a cargo of life-saving coal, however, they were fortunate to be dealing with a captain concerned more with humanity than the prospect of heavy profits.

AN HONEST QUAKER.

Many years ago during a severe winter, Nantucket harbor was frozen over for four weeks. The coal in store had long been exhausted, and there was much suffering from lack of fuel. Even the fences had been torn down and burnt to eke out the scanty supply of wood. To the great delight of the townspeople, the ice broke up one fine morning, and a schooner laden with coal was seen approaching. There was much excitement, and before the craft was moored, a coal dealer boarded her and eagerly addressed the honest Quaker skipper Gifford: "Wal, Cap'en," said he, "you've about hit it this cruise. I guess I'll hev to take y'ur hul cargo. Spose you'll want more'n the usual $7 a ton. Wal, I like to do the square thing by a friend, and I'll give you $12 a ton for it." "Friend," said Captain Gifford, "thee can have one ton of my coal if thee likes for $8, but only one ton, all must have a chance." Just then one of the richest men of the place joined them saying: "I want ten tons of your coal at your own price-name it. I have suffered enough for once." He received the same answer, and so did all-one ton for each family, and $8 as the price of each ton. No love of gain, no solicitation, no regard for individuals could move honest Captain Gifford.

Semi-Weekly Wisconsin, January 1, 1870.
Milwaukee, Wisconsin.

www.ingramcontent.com/pod-product-compliance
Lightning Source LLC
Chambersburg PA
CBHW020505030426
42337CB00011B/236